Indian Lives

Ulrich W. Hiesinger

INDIAN LIVES

A Photographic Record
from the Civil War
to Wounded Knee

With a foreword by
Joseph Medicine Crow

Prestel

Munich · New York

Front cover: *Brule Village near Pine Ridge,
South Dakota, 1891 (see pp. 120/21)*
Back cover: *Chief Whistling Elk, Fort Laramie,
Wyoming, 1868 (see pp. 80/81)*

Frontispiece: *Chiefs Spotted Tail, Roman Nose,
and Old Man Afraid of His Horses, Fort Laramie,
Wyoming, 1868 (see pp. 80/81)*

Prestel-Verlag

16 West 22nd Street, New York, NY 10010, USA
Tel. (212) 627 8199; Fax (212) 627 9866

Mandlstrasse 26, D-80802 Munich, Germany
Tel. (89) 381 7090; Fax (89) 381 70935

Distributed in Continental Europe by Prestel-Verlag
Verlegerdienst München GmbH & Co. KG
Gutenbergstrasse 1, D-82205 Gilching, Germany
Tel. (8105) 388 117, Fax (8105) 388 100

Distributed in the USA and Canada on behalf of Prestel
by te Neues Publishing Company,
16 West 22nd Street, New York, NY 10010, USA
Tel. (212) 627 9090; Fax (212) 627 9511

Distributed in Japan on behalf of Prestel by
YOHAN Western Publications Distribution Agency,
14-9 Okubo 3-chome, Shinjuku, J-Tokyo 169
Tel. (3) 32 08 01 81; Fax (3) 2 09 02 88

Distributed in the United Kingdom, Ireland and all
remaining countries on behalf of Prestel by
Thames & Hudson Ltd, 30-34 Bloomsbury Street,
London, WC1B 3QP, England
Tel. (71) 636 5488; Fax (71) 636 1659

Map by Wolfgang Mohrbach, Munich, Germany

Typeset by OK Satz GmbH, Unterschleissheim, Germany
Offset lithography by eurocrom 4, Villorba, Italy
Printed by Peradruck Matthias GmbH,
Gräfelfing near Munich, Germany
Bound by R. Oldenbourg GmbH, Munich, Germany

Printed in Germany

ISBN 3-7913-1422-X (English edition)
ISBN 3-7913-1516-5 (German edition)

CONTENTS

FOREWORD

One of my college professors used to say: "Don't read good books. There are too many good books around and life is too short to read them. Read only the best books." The volume before you belongs to the "best books" category. You must read it before you are too old.

Most pictorial books are ethno-historical, presenting a study of a particular ethnic group over a given period of time. This book accomplishes much more. It tells about the labors of many frontier photographers throughout the Indian country from c. 1861 to 1890, a period in American frontier history when many Indian tribes had already been exterminated, some were still in the process of being conquered, and some already had been subdued and placed in captivity on reservations.

The "shadow catchers" or "image makers" — names by which the early photographers were known to Indians — came right behind the early frontier painters, such as Karl Bodmer, George Catlin, Rudolph Kurz, and others, and carried on the documentation of the lives of the so-called "vanishing Americans." In fact, these pioneer picture-takers vastly improved upon the quality and quantity of pictorial recording of Indian life and history with the use of a new invention called the camera. No doubt some of these early photographers came into the Indian country as curiosity seekers, taking pictures of "savages" by means of the new apparatus. Inadvertently, and perhaps ironically, even they produced valuable ethnological material for posterity.

The work of identifying and compiling historical photographs represents an important contribution to American ethnology. Their presentation here provides the average reader with an almost instantaneous knowledge of Indians, something which many "good" books fail to do. Photographs of camp scenes, dances, ceremonials, and other situations and events reveal Indian cultures in action. The portraits of infants, adults, and octogenarians show a wide range of human emotions. The photographs reproduced here all convey explicit stories of human contentment or agitation, joy or sorrow, hope or despair, and other feelings and attitudes during a time when harsh acculturation was being forced upon the tribes. The narratives accompanying the images provide invaluable information. Serious students of Indian history and culture, both Indian and non-Indian, will find these very helpful, but the average reader about Indians will also enjoy them.

As the Historian/Anthropologist for my own Crow Indian Tribe of Montana, I sincerely appreciate the importance of this irreplaceable record. A scene showing the rimrocks of the Yellowstone Valley brings to mind what Chief Arapooish (Sore Belly) said to Robert Campbell of the American Fur Company in 1843: "The Crow Country is a good country because the Great Spirit has made it and put it in exactly the right place." Charles Milton Bell's classic portrait of my grandfather, Chief Medicine Crow, taken in Washington, D.C., in 1882 and illustrated in this book, reminds us of the long history of this "good country," which extends into the present.

On behalf of my own Crow Tribe I say AHO, AHO (Thank you, thank you) for this book. I am sure many other tribal people will join me in this expression of gratitude.

JOSEPH MEDICINE CROW
Crow Tribal Historian/Anthropologist

ACKNOWLEDGMENTS

Sincere thanks are owed to the following individuals for their generous help in providing information and/or assistance in obtaining photographs: Helen M. Plummer, Amon Carter Museum, Fort Worth; Casey Barthelmess; George Miles, Beinecke Rare Book and Manuscript Library, Yale University; Eric Paddock, Colorado Historical Society; Sarah Erwin, Gilcrease Museum, Tulsa; Brita Mack, Huntington Library; Prof. Raymond J. DeMallie, Indiana University; Bonnie Wilson and Tracey Baker, Minnesota Historical Society; Peter J. Michel, Missouri Historical Society; Becca Kohl, Montana Historical Society; Richard Rudisill, Museum of New Mexico; Laura Nash, National Museum of the American Indian, Smithsonian Institution; John Carter and Martha Vestecka-Miller, Nebraska State Historical Society; Margaret Kulis and Meg Bolger, The Newberry Library, Chicago; Anne Wilson and Molly Haberman, W. H. Over Museum, University of South Dakota; Errol Stevens, Seavers Center for Western History Research, Los Angeles; Mary Elizabeth Ruwell and Paula Fleming, National Anthropological Archives, Smithsonian Institution; Donna M. Greene, Smithsonian Institution; Melanie Brown Rout and Denise Bethel, Sotheby's, New York; Ligia Perez, The Southwest Museum, Los Angeles; Joe McGregor, U.S. Geological Survey, Denver; and Robert M. Utley.

A special note of thanks is owed to Joseph Medicine Crow, Crow Tribal Historian/Anthropologist, for his sincere and generous support.

Seattle

WASHINGTON

PACIFIC
OCEAN

Yakima

Cayuse

Umatilla

Nez Perce

OREGON

Boise

IDAHO

Blackfoot

Piegan

Gros Ventre

Missouri River

Helena

Jordan

MONTANA

Yellowstone River

✗ Big Hole
1877

Bozeman

Little Bighorn ✗
1876

Crow

Fetterma
Fight 18

*Yellowstone
National Park*

Fort
Phil Kearny

Bighorn River

Powder Riv

Modoc

Northern Paiute

Shoshoni

Central Pacific Railroad

Promontory
Point

▲ South Pass

WYOMING

Fort Larami

San Francisco

*Pyramid
Lake*

Carson City

NEVADA

*Great
Salt Lake*

Salt Lake
City

Snake River

Union Pacific Railroad

Cheyen

UTAH

Ute

Denve

COLORADO

Southern
Paiute

CALIFORNIA

Las Vegas

PACIFIC
OCEAN

Havasupai

Mojave

Los Angeles

Navajo

Canyon de Chelly
1864

Hopi ⬟ Navajo Agency

Colorado River

Tao

Santa Fe

Rio Grande
Pueblos

ARIZONA

Zuni

NEW MEXICO

Bosque Redon
Age

Phoenix

San Carlos
Agency

Yuma

Chiricahua
Apache

Mescalero
Apache

Pima

Rio Grande

MEXICO

El Paso

Seattle

San
Francisco

New York

Washington

Houston

New Orleans

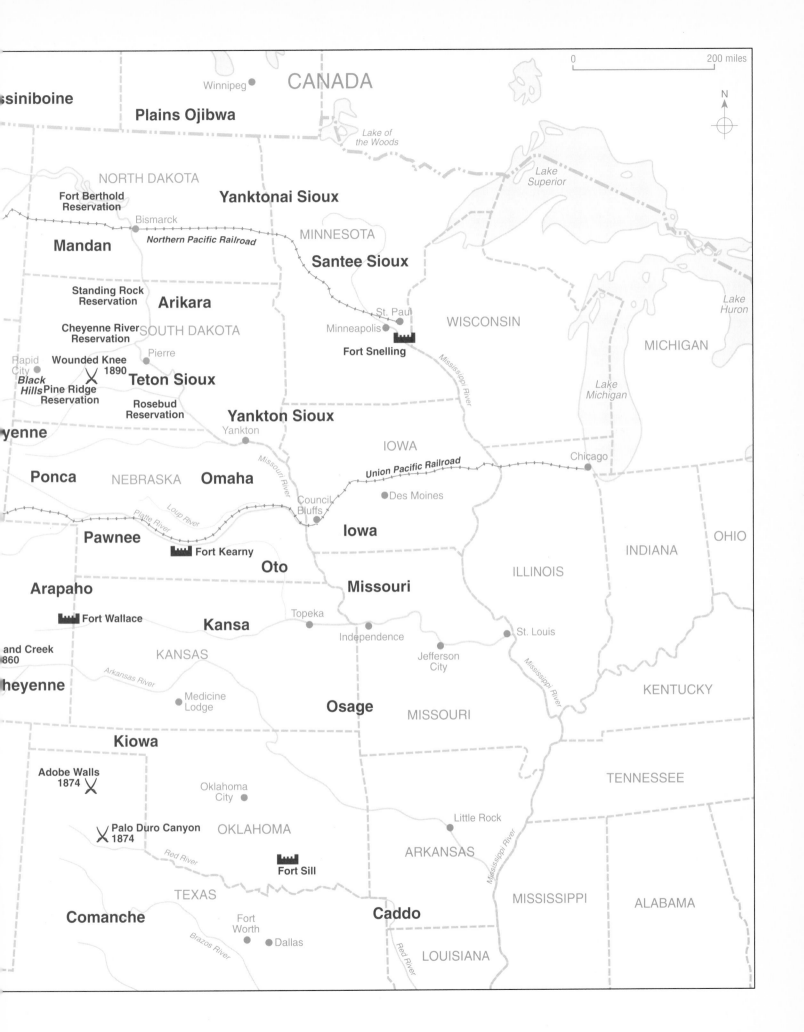

ssiniboine

Plains Ojibwa

CANADA

Winnipeg

Lake of the Woods

Lake Superior

NORTH DAKOTA

Yanktonai Sioux

Fort Berthold
Reservation

Bismarck

Northern Pacific Railroad

MINNESOTA

Mandan

Santee Sioux

Standing Rock
Reservation

Arikara

St. Paul

WISCONSIN

Lake Huron

Cheyenne River
Reservation

SOUTH DAKOTA

Minneapolis

MICHIGAN

Pierre

Fort Snelling

Rapid
City

Wounded Knee
1890

*Black
Hills* Pine Ridge
Reservation

Teton Sioux

Mississippi River

*Lake
Michigan*

yenne

Rosebud
Reservation

Yankton Sioux

Yankton

IOWA

Chicago

Ponca

NEBRASKA

Omaha

Missouri River

Union Pacific Railroad

OHIO

Council
Bluffs

Des Moines

Pawnee

Platte River

Loup River

Fort Kearny

Iowa

INDIANA

Oto

Arapaho

Missouri

ILLINOIS

Fort Wallace

Kansa

Topeka

St. Louis

and Creek
860

KANSAS

Independence

Mississippi River

heyenne

Arkansas River

Jefferson
City

KENTUCKY

Medicine
Lodge

Osage

MISSOURI

Kiowa

Adobe Walls
1874

Oklahoma
City

TENNESSEE

Palo Duro Canyon
1874

OKLAHOMA

Little Rock

Red River

ARKANSAS

Mississippi River

Fort Sill

TEXAS

MISSISSIPPI

ALABAMA

Comanche

Fort
Worth

Caddo

Brazos River

Dallas

Red River

LOUISIANA

0   200 miles

N

11

PHOTOGRAPHING THE WESTERN FRONTIER, c. 1865-1890

The Great Spirit has made this country for us, and has put buffalo and game in it for us, but the white man come and build roads and drive off the game, and we and our children starve. I love my children as you, white man, love yours, and when I see them starving, it makes my heart black, and I am angry. We are glad to have the traders, but we don't want you soldiers and roadmakers; the country is ours and we intend to keep it; tell the Great Father we won't sell it, and tell him to keep his soldiers at home.

Sioux Elder, 1860

One of the most striking aspects about the conquest of the American West, and one which no thoughtful person failed to observe, was the astonishing speed with which it was accomplished. In 1872 the frontier traveler Francis Parkman recalled a time some twenty-five years earlier when, riding by the foot of Pike's Peak with a companion, he had reflected on a future that would bring an end to the life and country they had visited, when the Plains would be turned into pasture and cattle would replace the buffalo, and when the wolves, bears, and Indians that inhabited the wild country would be a thing of the past. "We knew that more and more, year after year, the trains of emigrant wagons would creep in slow procession towards barbarous Oregon or wild and distant California; but we did not dream how Commerce and Gold would breed nations along the Pacific, the disenchanting screech of the locomotive break the spell of weird mysterious mountains, woman's rights invade the fastnesses of the Arapahoes, and despairing savagery, assailed in front and rear, vail its scalp-locks and feathers before triumphant commonplace."

Neither pen nor brush nor camera was quick enough to document many aspects of Native American culture that disappeared during the final phase of white expansion, between the end of the Civil War in 1865 and the last

major armed conflict between Indians and whites, at Wounded Knee in 1890. Before that, Indian lands east of the Mississippi and, more recently, in California and the Pacific Northwest, had already come under white dominion, leaving the Great Plains and the Southwest as the last dwindling retreat of the free Indian. When the Civil War ended, emigration westward exploded. Emigrants who had once passed through the center of the country now began to settle on lands formerly considered useless for farming, and to mine the hills for newly discovered minerals. Steamboats plied the rivers, the railroads blasted away mountain sides, and boom towns sprang up in a matter of weeks or months, choking the valleys with frame buildings where virgin forest had stood. Thus, towns, mills, mines, and farms permanently changed the land, driving out the game animals and, with them, the native inhabitants. This profusion of giant structures and fabulous inventions demonstrated at once the white settlers' power and their completely alien attitude toward the land.

Prior to the advent of photography a number of American and European artists had worked on the frontier recording the native cultures that, even in the early nineteenth century, were threatened with extinction. None was more active than the painter George Catlin who, inspired by the thought that such ancient peoples still

existed in their original habitat, resolved to go west and "rescue from oblivion so much of their primitive looks and customs as the industry and ardent enthusiasm of one lifetime could accomplish." During visits to many Plains tribes in the 1830s, he sat in councils, rode on buffalo hunts, observed games, dances, and religious ceremonies, and painted many hundreds of pictures of individuals, as well as scenes of hunting and domestic life. In the second half of the nineteenth century, before the frontier finally vanished, there was no single artist

---

Medicine Crow or Sacred Raven (Perits-Shinakpas), Crow tribe, 1880. Albumen print by Charles Milton Bell. Among the greatest Crow warriors of his era, Medicine Crow was also esteemed as a visionary medicine man. He gained his first fighting experience when fifteen years old, on an 1863 expedition against the Shoshonis; at the age of twenty-two he was made war chief. His numerous deeds in battles against the Shoshonis, Sioux, and Arapahos, many involving hand-to-hand combat, became legendary. As allies of the U.S. Army forces, he and his warriors fought against the Sioux at the battle of Rosebud in 1876 and against the Nez Perces in 1877. The distinctive treatment of Medicine Crow's hair, with long locks at side and back and a stiff, upswept "pompadour" in front, was prevalent among the Crows, the Nez Perces, and one or two other western tribes.

Valley of the Yellowstone, looking south from the first canyon, 1871. Albumen print by William Henry Jackson.
More than anything else, Americans were curious to experience through paintings and photographs the majestic landscapes of the western frontier. Lieutenant Henry E. Maynadier, who reconnoitered the Yellowstone Valley with the Raynolds expedition in 1860, observed its vast herds of buffalo, antelope, and elk and described it as "the paradise of the Indian." In 1872 the Yellowstone was designated America's first national park.

or photographer who could match Catlin's dedication. Instead, the documentation that does exist came about in random fashion from a variety of photographers working either privately or for government surveys. Their photographs often reveal how Indian culture was being altered daily by contact with white civilization. This was especially apparent in the western dress adopted wholly or partly by more

and more Native Americans and in the trade items, such as woven cloth, beads, and iron utensils, that replaced or transformed objects of traditional handcraft. Yet there was still much to be appreciated of original cultures, even as they were fast changing or disappearing. With an immediacy and detail only possible in photography, a visual record has survived of many unique aspects of traditional Indian dwellings, dress, occupations, and ceremonies. Some photographs, such as those taken at the 1868 Fort Laramie council or at the battlefield of Wounded Knee, record great historic events. Others preserve the likenesses of Indian leaders made famous in the frontier wars. Still others bring to life the small but precious details of daily life and capture the images of anonymous individuals of all ages and both genders. Together, they tell of continuity as well as change among native peoples, of poverty and suffering as well as great strength and physical beauty.

The photographic record of Indian life began soon after photography was invented, as itinerant daguerreotypists followed the settlements westward. In 1847 Thomas Easterly created a memorable series of portraits of Indian leaders at St. Louis, then at the edge of the frontier, and in the early 1850s John Fitzgibbon visited Indian settlements in southwest Missouri to take a group of portrait daguerreotypes that was exhibited with great

Emigrants' wagon train passing through Echo Canyon, Utah, 1866/67. Albumen print on a C. W. Carter mount, but attributed to Charles R. Savage. Those who rode the wave of westward migration after the Civil War wrested control of Indian land at an increasing rate. Telegraph poles can already be seen along this well-traveled route. In 1869, at Promontory Point, seventy-five miles northwest of where this picture was taken, the first transcontinental railroad was completed.

success at the New York Crystal Palace Exhibition in 1853. A curious broadside of 1854 advertising the services of the daguerreotypist Talmadge Elwell in St. Anthony, Minnesota, encouraged all to have their portraits taken, declaring that "even the 'Sons Of The Forest' shall be received with that consideration due to their rank as NATIVE AMERICANS." Whether Elwell really hoped to lure Indians as paying clients is not known, but in general the interest shown by studio photographers in images of Native Americans was due mainly to their novelty and to the attention they attracted.

Leaders of the expeditions sent to explore and survey the West were quick to realize the importance of photography in recording and advertising their projects. There were attempts as early as the 1840s to include photographers on these expeditions, although none of their work has survived. The first significant results apparently came during the 1853 expedition of John Charles Frémont, who hired the photographer Solomon Nunes Carvalho to record his journey through the Rocky Mountains. Carvalho wrote an interesting account of his experiences, describing how he was forced to adapt the daguerreotype process to the severe conditions of western travel, including one instance in which he buffed and coated his plates while standing up to his waist in snow. He attempted to make daguerreotypes of a huge buffalo herd on the move, but failed owing to the long exposures required; he did succeed, however, in taking several of distant herds. In Montana he took a series of pictures in a Cheyenne village, among them some portraits of inhabitants. One he particularly remembered was of a chief's daughter, whom he described as "a beautiful Indian girl [who] attired herself in her most costly robes, ornamented with elk teeth, beads, and colored porcupine quills — expressly to have her likeness taken. I made a beautiful

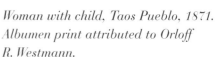

Woman with child, Taos Pueblo, 1871. Albumen print attributed to Orloff R. Westmann.

18

Chief Washakie's village, Shoshoni, 1870. Original negative by William Henry Jackson.
The view of this camp of nearly one hundred lodges was taken in autumn at South Pass, near the Sweetwater River. The Shoshonis, wrote the photographer, "were on their way to the Wind River Valley to hunt buffalo for the winter's supply of food and clothing. Although the village had all the appearance of being a permanent abiding-place, yet the following morning, before the sun was an hour high, there was not a tent in sight, and the last pack-pony with trailing lodge poles had passed out of sight over the hills to the eastward."

picture of her." Carvalho was forced to leave the expedition in February 1854 at Parowan, Utah, nearly dead from hunger and exposure. His daguerreotypes were later copied in Mathew Brady's Washington studio, but both the originals and the copies were destroyed in a warehouse fire. Only one picture survives that may be credibly attributed to Carvalho— an obscure image of some Plains tipis.

Other early photographs of Native American subjects were taken on the British-sponsored expedition of Henry Youle Hind to the Great Lakes area in 1857/58 and by the artist Albert Bierstadt while he was traveling in Kansas and Nebraska with the expedition of Colonel Frederick West Lander in 1859. Captain William Franklin Raynolds's 1859/60 expedition to the Yellowstone region and the Wind River Mountains also produced a few rare views of Indian subjects, as did the joint American-British Northwest Boundary Survey of 1860-62.

In Washington, D.C., photographic records of Indian delegations began to be produced as early as

1852. Starting in the fall of 1857, the James E. McClees gallery attempted to take photographs of all the Indian delegates who came to the capital. A number of these images, including several of the famous Chief Little Crow, have survived, but the project lasted less than a year, and it was not until the later 1860s that the practice was revived, in the belief that the Indian was fast disappearing and ought to be recorded. In 1867 the first regular program of recording delegations was undertaken by the Smithsonian Institution.

In the years between 1867 and 1879 four great geographical and geological surveys were initiated by the government to explore and chart the largely unknown regions west of the Mississippi. Photography played an important part in recording and promoting these surveys and several of the best known American photographers were involved: Timothy H. O'Sullivan, in the King and Wheeler surveys (1867-79 and 1871-79); William Henry Jackson, in the Hayden Survey (1870-79); and Edward O. Beaman and John K. Hillers, in the Powell Survey (1871-79). In addition to photographing their group's operations and features of the landscape, they produced a significant body of photographs of Indians encountered along the way.

Working on their own, private photographers in search of new material also belonged to the process of exploration engaged in by organized parties, and it is to them that we owe an equal, if not greater, part of the most original work. Jackson actually first joined the Hayden Survey in 1870 as an unpaid photographer, expecting to earn his way by the sale of his pictures alone. His adventurous spirit was already evidenced in the late 1860s when, as a private practitioner in Omaha, Nebraska, he regularly rode out with his traveling darkroom to photograph the various tribes of Osage, Oto,

Keokuk (One Who Moves About Alert) of the Sauk and Fox, 1847. Daguerreotype by Thomas M. Easterly.
Born at about the time of the American Revolution, Keokuk was among the earliest Native American leaders to be photographed. This daguerreotype was made at St. Louis, which was then the jumping off point for the western frontier. During Keokuk's lifetime, U.S. territory expanded across the entire continent, from the Alleghanies to the Pacific Ocean.

Pawnee, Winnebago, Omaha, and Ponca Indians who lived within reach of the city. Jackson had to overcome some initial reluctance among the Indians, but "soon," he said, "my one-horse studio (which at first scared the daylights out of the livestock) ceased to be considered 'bad medicine,' and I was welcomed equally before the tee-pees of the Poncas and the earthen houses of the Pawnees." Jackson hired his subjects to pose by the hour and sold his pictures both in local stores and through dealers in the East. The most profitable outlet for such material was in the form of stereographs — images, produced by a dual-lensed camera in imitation of human vision, that give an illusion of three-dimensionality when viewed through a stereoscope. As a popular home entertainment in the later nineteenth century, stereographs of distant places and peoples were sold widely in sets; hence, most photographers traveled with at least one double-lensed stereo camera. Government expeditions and their members benefited from this trade, both the Wheeler and Powell surveys, for example, producing stereographs for commercial sale. Powell, we know, shared the proceeds with photographers Hillers and Thompson. Hillers's stereo images with a U.S. Department of the Interior label on the back reportedly netted $4,000 in the first six months of their being on sale.

Fish trap and buckskin lodges, c. 1860-62. Albumen print by an unknown photographer.
One of the rare images of Native American life taken in the field prior to the Civil War, this photograph was shot on the Northwest Boundary Survey, a joint American-Canadian venture. Some of the tipis are a composite type utilizing skins and brush.

Plains Indians referred to photographers in general as "shadow catchers," while the Utes, alluding to a picture's resemblance to a reflection, gave Hillers the name "Myself in the Water." The attitudes of Native Americans unfamiliar with the technology of photography varied from casual acceptance to suspicion and out-

right fear. Dr. Ferdinand Vandiveer Hayden noted in 1877 that the latter stemmed from a belief that securing an image would somehow place some part of the subject under the control of the photographer. There were some chiefs, he said, whom no amount of persuasion could induce to have their photograph taken. Evidence of this

is provided by Jackson's description of an incident at the Los Pinos Agency in 1874 when he was challenged by a group of Utes who believed that having their pictures taken would cause them to become sick and die. Jackson set up his camera inside a cookhouse, hoping to shoot surreptitiously through the doorway; on discovering this, one of

◁ Chippewa (Ojibwa) craftsmen making birch-bark canoes, Minnesota, 1880. Frame from an albumen stereograph by Charles A. Zimmerman.
In an era marked both by change and by the continuation of ancient traditions, western-style clothing was adopted by those still pursuing the age-old craft of canoe-making typical of northern woodlands tribes. In the background are seen rounded wigwams covered in birch bark.

Ute warrior with bride, August 1, 1871. Albumen print by Edward O. Beaman.
When encountered by the Powell expedition in July 1871, the warrior and his bride were in hiding. The young Gray Eagle, son of Douglass, chief of the White River Utes, had eloped with a Uinta chief's daughter (Pi-Av — Honey Dew of the Mountains) who was already betrothed to another man. Custom required the lapse of a certain amount of time for such a union to be legitimized and for the couple to be allowed to return to their people.

The menacing show of arms was no doubt put on for the camera, but the body paint and splendid costumes seem to have been a genuine part of their nuptial celebration.

the Indians tried to charge inside on horseback and, joined by a group of others, blocked the doorway with a blanket until Jackson gave up. Figures in a fair number of photographs can be seen hiding from the camera, and more than one photographer's life was threatened for attempting to take pictures.

Further obstacles were imposed by the technology of photography. During most of the period in question, photographers employed the wet-plate process, which came into general use about 1860. Its major advantage over the daguerreotype, which produced a unique image on a metal plate, was that it

used glass negatives, from which an unlimited number of paper prints could be produced. It was especially burdensome in the field, however, since it involved a complex and delicate process whereby a glass plate was covered with a light-sensitive compound that required exposing and developing while the plate was still wet. Premature drying or contamination by fingerprints, dust, or dirty water could ruin the plate. In addition to being fragile, the glass plates were extremely heavy when

Corn Dance, also known as Tablita Dance, at Cochiti Pueblo, New Mexico, July 1888. Original negative by Charles F. Lummis.

Rows of dancers, about eighty in all, took part in the ceremonial dance, which lasted seven hours. The men, their bare chests painted in red or blue, wore leggings and a dancing skirt with a sash and fox skin. Each held a sprig of evergreen and a gourd rattle. The women wore flat headboards called *tablitas*, their designs indicating membership in the Turquoise and Squash *kivas*. To the right, in front of the grouped chorus, are several clowns painted with clay. Although able to take pictures on this occasion, Lummis was refused permission by Pueblo officials to photograph the same dance three years later.

carried in quantity. Photographers were encumbered with a large array of chemicals, glass plates, and cameras, as well as with portable darkrooms.

The equipment carried by Jackson in the 1875 season, for example, included three different cameras and lenses, tripods, a dark tent, quantities of chemicals, such as collodion, silver nitrate, iron sulfate, and potassium cyanide, together with alcohol, varnish, bottles, developing and fixing trays, scales, and, not least, four hundred sheets of glass. Similar equipment carried by Beaman on the Powell Survey of the Grand Canyon was

A Sioux warrior's grave, Timber Creek (near present-day Jordan), Montana, 1879. Frame from an original stereograph negative by Laton Alton Huffman.

In accordance with ancient custom, the body of the dead warrior, along with his favorite possessions, was wrapped in blankets and placed on a scaffold raised to the sky on rough wooden posts. The photographer, who happened on the scene in winter, recalled: "The grave was new, its occupant having been killed but a few days. The site overlooked a vast plain, checkered with trails and dotted with moving herds of buffalo."

Northern house block, Acoma Pueblo, New Mexico, c. 1885. Albumen print by Ben Wittick.
Situated on a high mesa, Acoma survived as one of the oldest continuously inhabited sites in North America, dating back to at least the twelfth century. Each of the terraced adobe houses had its own rounded oven for baking bread, with stacks of firewood nearby. Meat and vegetables, hung on racks, are left drying in the sun.

referred to as "the terror of the party" by an expedition member who noted that cameras, darkroom, and boxes of chemicals and glass plates often had to be dragged up heights ranging from five hundred to three thousand feet.

The amount of equipment, and the time it took to set up the cameras, meant that it was virtually impossible to photograph subjects spontaneously, just as the long exposure times required subjects to remain still, since even slight movements — often encountered with dogs, horses, or even trees moving in the wind — resulted in a blurring of the image.

Widespread fighting throughout the era obliged photographers to attach themselves to organized parties or to stay fairly close to established towns or military forts. Some, such as William S. Soule, Christian Barthelmess, and Laton Huffman, operated studios at military posts, where taking pictures of army personnel provided the mainstay of their business and where they were able to photograph those Indians drawn their way by the course of military events.

Travel outside such protected enclaves was liable to be dangerous and unpredictable. In 1862 the photographer Adrian Ebell and his assistant Edwin R. Lawton made a journey up the Mississippi to southeast Minnesota "for the purpose of obtaining views of Indians and scenery." They were at the Upper Agency of the Santee Sioux reservation in August when fighting broke out around them in what proved to be the bloodiest Indian uprising in U.S. history. Ebell is credited with taking the only "action" photograph of the historic conflict, though it was a view not of actual combat, but of a group of refugees camped on the prairie during their flight toward safety. His inability to photograph any of the action itself demonstrated the virtual impossibility

of photographing fast-moving events in a combat zone without fixed lines.

The photographer Ridgway Glover was likewise thrust into the center of frontier fighting and ultimately became one of its tragic victims. An impulsive and eccentric character, Glover was a Philadelphia Quaker of some means who had devoted himself to photography and to the study of Native American life. He went west in the summer of 1866, determined to visit all the frontier territories and take views on his route across the Rocky Mountains. In a series of letters published under the title "Photog-

Crow winter encampment, Montana, 1870s or 1880s. Frame from an albumen stereograph by Calfee & Catlin. The remoteness of many wandering tribes made such views as this extremely difficult to capture. This unusual scene of a winter settlement shows several of the camp's inhabitants bundled against the cold and a group of dogs stirring about in the snow. Stacks of firewood are piled outside the tightly closed tipis, at the bases of which snow is banked to help keep out drafts. To the right is a shield tripod which, in heraldic fashion, served to identify the lodge's owner.

raphy Among the Indians" in the magazine *Philadelphia Photographer* he described his experiences in the West. However brief, this is one of the most vivid accounts of the opportunities and hindrances facing the frontier photographer.

Glover arrived in June 1866 at Fort Laramie, Wyoming, to witness the great gathering of Sioux, Arapaho, and Cheyenne who had been invited by government Commissioners trying to negotiate a peace treaty to ensure safe passage for travelers along the Bozeman Trail. The political occasion seemed to interest Glover only insofar as it offered him subject matter for photographs. Muddy water spoiled over half his negatives but, by the end of the month, he said that he had obtained twenty-two good negatives, which he promised to send back east with the returning Peace Commissioners. He declared: "I had much difficulty in making pictures of the Indians at first, but now I am able to talk to them, yet I get pretty much all I want . . . . Some of the Sioux think photography is 'pazuta zupa' (bad medicine). Today I was over trying to take the Wahcopomony at the great Brulie Sioux village. The wind blew so hard I could not make but one passable negative, though I had some of the most interesting scenes imaginable. Here the division of the presents from the Government was made and some 1200 Sioux were arranged, squatting around the Commissioners in a large circle, three rows deep. The village embraces more than 200 tribes (lodges) led by 'Spotted Tail.' 'Standing Elk,' 'The Man that walks under the ground,' and 'Running Bear'. 'The Man that walks under the ground' is a good friend of mine. He and the 'Run-

ning Bear' have had their pictures taken. I have been introduced to the other two and they are friendly. So I took all I chose, or rather all I could after the wind subsided towards the evening. The camp presented a lively scene. They have just moved it up to the junction of the Platte and Laramie on the north side of the Platte, and arranged it so as to inclose a half mile inside their tents to secure their horses, which they herd in the day-time, and drive in at night. Some 500 ponies were pasturing around, and the scene

Navajo family group with woman at a ▷
loom, Canyon de Chelly, New Mexico Territory, 1873. Frame from an albumen stereograph by Timothy O'Sullivan.
The photographer took this view illustrating "Aboriginal Life" while a member of the Wheeler Geographical Survey, carried out under Lieutenant George M. Wheeler, from 1871 to 1873. It is particularly interesting for its illustration of the blanket loom suspended from two large tree trunks. Navajo woven blankets were coveted by neighboring tribes for their exceptional quality and imperviousness to rain.

◁ *Apache family bathing, Ojo Caliente, New Mexico, 1889. Albumen print by Dana B. Chase.*
This unique family portrait shows Antonio Monyes and his wife Suyh with Mannaha, Touce, and another of their children. The ancient mineral springs near the family's home were famous for their healing powers.

was novel and beautiful, with the river on the south . . . . Towards night, about 100 Indians came out on horseback, and I witnessed three match races of about as fast horse traveling as I wish to see, and the riders far wilder than the horses. Some of the Indians think they will die in three days, if they get their pictures taken. At the ferry to-day I pointed the instrument at one of that opinion. The poor fellow fell on the sand, and rolled himself in his blanket. The most of them know

better, though, and some I have made understand that the light comes from the sun, strikes them, and then goes into the machine. I explained it to one yesterday, by means of his looking glass, and showed him an image on the ground glass. When he caught the idea, he brightened up, and was willing to stand for me. I make them Ferrotypes, and put brass around them, and they think they are *wash-ta-le-poka*. (Their superlative for good)."

31

Glover next went north to the Powder River country, where the party of soldiers he was traveling with was attacked by Indians. Retreating to a hilltop, they managed to hold off their attackers until help arrived. Glover said of the incident: "[The Indians] looked very wild and savage-like while galloping around us; and I desired to make some instantaneous views, but our commander ordered me not to, as he expected an attack at any time." Further along the journey his party was attacked once more and, when he finally arrived at his destination at Fort Phil Kearny, Glover reported with barely concealed excitement: "[I] arrived here, at the base of a mountain whose summit is surrounded perpetually with a wreath of purest snow. I am surrounded by beautiful scenery, and hemmed in by yelling savages, who are surprising and killing some one every day. I expect to get some good pictures here." At the end of August he was still at Fort Kearny, living in a log house with a company of woodchoppers. He had run out of photographic chemicals and was waiting for a medical supply train to bring more. One day in the middle of September he went out on his own, either to take some views or to make sketches. Met in the field by Indian raiders, he was killed, scalped, and "horribly mutilated." No trace of Glover's frontier photographs has ever come to light.

It is clear both that the quality of photographs with Native American subjects varied greatly and that our appreciation of them does not always reflect their original purpose. For instance, one otherwise interesting photograph of 1866, showing three Omaha chiefs in native dress, bears the printed caption "Uneducated Indian Chiefs." There are also countless stiffly posed studio portraits with painted backdrops and papier-mâché rocks,

Pedro Jose Quivera, governor of San Felipe Pueblo, demonstrating the use of the traditional bow drill, 1880. Albumen print by John K. Hillers.

*Photographer Adrian Ebell and his
assistant Edwin R. Lawton working
from a boat in Minnesota, 1862.
Albumen print by an unknown photographer.
Lawton is seen working in a portable
darkroom.*

as well as studio tableaux in which
Indians act out sham battles or halt
in the midst of some imagined
dance. Such theatrics are easily
recognizable and understandable as
part of the histrionic tradition that
governed contemporary oratory and
stagecraft. More insidious, however, were certain cases in which
political or commercial pressures
led to outright misrepresentation.
An example occurred during the
Modoc War of 1872/73 when,
unable to record scenes of actual
combat, a photographer resorted to
posing an allied Indian scout with

his rifle, which he then labeled "A Modoc Warrior on the Warpath." The offender was no less a photographer than Eadweard Muybridge, and the image was reproduced for a national audience in *Harper's Weekly*.

Another instance involved the explorer and government ethnographer John Wesley Powell. In the summer of 1873, evidently eager to have something to show for his trouble, and concerned about continued funding for his activities, Powell arranged to have photographs taken of Ute Indians dressed in costumes supplied for the occasion. Some were genuine Indian clothes, as the Smithsonian accession number still visible on one buckskin dress demonstrates. However, other items of so-called Indian clothing, including feather headdresses, had been manufactured the previous year under the direction of Powell's sister, Ellen Thompson, and were now used to dress up a band of Kanab Paiutes who were apparently considered insufficiently picturesque in their impoverished, tattered condition. To this masquerade was added the artistic talents of the painter Thomas Moran, who helped arrange "effective attitudes" for the Indian subjects. Today, these images are a painful reminder of how political and/or commercial pressures could distort the accuracy of the photographic record. The most genuine feature of the photographs is the clear sense of discomfort among many of the Indian subjects, whose attitudes and miserable looks express quite unmistakably their unwilling participation in the fraud.

By the end of the era, having experienced white interference in their religious ceremonies, many Native Americans had become less willing to be photographed under any circumstances. This was true of some Pueblo Indians, as well as of those who performed the Ghost Dance, which had been outlawed by the government, on the Pine Ridge and other reservations. At the same time, the introduction of light, hand-held cameras in the 1880s greatly facilitated the taking of photographs quickly and unobtrusively in the field. The ethnologist James Mooney recognized the new potential during his field study of the Ghost Dance religion in 1890 and secured some of the most moving portrayals of American Indian life ever recorded. When he first arrived at the Pine Ridge reservation to learn about the Ghost Dance, no one would speak to him about it. "The dance was our religion," the Sioux told him, "but the government sent soldiers to kill us on account of it. We will not talk any more about it." Among the Kiowas, Arapahos, Cheyennes, and other tribes, however, Mooney was able to gain the confidence of the organizers and to observe and record the dance at first hand while other whites were being ordered away. Still, he felt that it was dangerous to advertise himself with the cumbersome tripod camera he had brought, and sent for a manual so that he could learn to use his portable Kodak. By photographing the Ghost Dance, Mooney challenged the government's efforts to suppress certain native customs that it considered dangerous and, at one point, he was warned that, if he pursued his work contrary to the Commissioner's orders, he would be arrested and expelled from the reservation. This kind of attempted censorship ran counter to the interests of photographers, scholars, and an increasingly inquisitive public. After the massacre at Wounded Knee, George H. Harries, correspondent for the *Washington Star*, reported on February 1, 1891: "About the last of the busy sojourners to leave Pine Ridge were the photographers . . . . It was hard work to supply the local demand for the pictures they took and for quite a while impossible to fill the orders that tumbled in from all parts of the country."

Whistling Elk, one of the chiefs who signed the Fort Laramie treaty ending the Powder River War, flanked by Lone Horn and Pipe, 1868. Albumen print by Alexander Gardner (detail).

STANLEY J. MORROW:
A PHOTOGRAPHER'S TRAVELS

Stanley J. Morrow, age nineteen, in the uniform of the Seventh Wisconsin Iron Brigade, 1862. Albumen print by an unknown photographer.

As a young recruit during the Civil War, Stanley J. Morrow fought in several major battles before a disability gave him the opportunity to learn photograph, under Mathew Brady. After the war he moved with his wife to Yankton, Dakota Territory, where he built a home and studio. With Yankton as his operating base, he spent the years 1869 to 1881 traveling the length of the Missouri River and its tributaries in the Dakota and Montana territories in search of photographic subjects. He stopped for weeks or months at a time at various towns and army posts, improvising a studio for the portraits of local residents that formed the mainstay of his business. Separate excursions along his route were made to photograph landscapes and scenes from Indian life, which became his special preoccupation. Included in his work are photographs of the Sioux, Cheyenne, Crow, Arikara, Mandan, Hidatsa, Ponca, Assiniboine, and Bannock tribes.

On his travels he was sometimes accompanied by his wife, Isa, and even by their small child. In wandering through wild and hostile country, Morrow endured extremes of summer heat, blinding prairie snowstorms, and the constant threat of Indian attack. Often the danger from Indians was based on nothing more than wild stories, but at times it was real enough. On one expedition he and his wife were besieged in a cabin for several days by Indian raiders, and during another tense encounter he was shot at by an Indian guarding a burial ground that Morrow had hoped to photograph.

Typical of Morrow's extensive journeys was one that lasted from May 1870 until the following January, during which time he traveled nine hundred miles by riverboat and five hundred overland. He prospered along the way, but rewards were neither certain nor secure. In November 1872, for example, after

Morrow's photographic gallery and home in Yankton, Dakota Territory, 1869. Albumen print by Stanley J. Morrow.
Morrow's wife, Isa, and the couple's two young daughters appear in the doorway of the building, which featured a large skylight and glass-walled studio.

one of several long working stays in Helena, Montana, he returned home penniless after being robbed of $800 while on a sleeping car of the Northern Pacific Railroad.

In 1876 Morrow took photographs of the burgeoning mining towns in the Black Hills that provoked the Sioux war, and had some of them published in New York newspapers. That fall, he also photographed scenes during General George Crook's campaign against the Sioux and views of the famous Custer battlefield.

In 1878 he undertook his last major photographic expedition — which lasted nearly a year and a half — in order to complete a stereographic series that he titled "Photographic Gems of the Great Northwest." Returning to Yankton, he built a new brick studio in 1880, but used it only a short time before moving permanently to the South in 1883. An advertisement placed by Morrow in the *Yankton Press* before he left provided a first-hand summary of his career, offering as it did "views taken by me during an experience of twelve years on the frontier, involving great personal dangers, expense and hardships. I have spent considerable time among

the hostile Sioux, and have on several occasions nearly lost my scalp, in endeavors to secure some particular view. I represent sixteen bands of the Sioux Nation, all but three of them being termed hostile Sioux."

A makeshift studio of canvas, lean-to timbers, and glass panes, Fort Wadsworth (now Sisseton), Dakota Territory, 1870. Albumen print by Stanley J. Morrow.

View of Rapid City, Dakota Territory, with Morrow's portable darkroom and field equipment in the foreground, 1876. Albumen print by Stanley J. Morrow.
When working closer to home, Morrow also used a specially designed wagon as a portable darkroom.

MINNESOTA UPRISING, 1862

The Indians wanted to live as they did before the treaty of Traverse des Sioux — go where they pleased and when they pleased; hunt game wherever they could find it, sell their furs to the traders, and live as they could.

Chief Big Eagle (Wambde Tonka), Santee Sioux

In the 1850s the Santee Sioux in present-day Minnesota sold most of their lands — a total of almost twenty-four million acres — to the government and, for about a decade thereafter, lived peaceably on two narrow reservations along the Minnesota River, dependent on government annuities for their support. By the winter of 1861/62 crop failures had brought the Indians near to starvation. The annuity payment was late in coming the next summer, and without it the Indians could not buy food. In July 1862 some five thousand hungry Sioux arrived at their reservation's Upper Agency and asked that food be issued to them from the government warehouses. This was done, but the Indians came back on August 4, surrounded a military guard of about one hundred soldiers, and began carrying off provisions for themselves. Again, it was arranged to give them food in advance of annuity payments, and the Sioux returned to their homes. These and other confrontations set the stage for a brief, but extremely bloody, conflict that heralded nearly thirty years of warfare between Native Americans and white settlers west of the Mississippi.

One of the Santee Sioux leaders, Big Eagle, described the circumstances that led to the Minnesota Uprising. There was resentment among the Indians, he said, because the white authorities did not allow them to go to war against their enemies and pressured them to give up their old life for work as farmers. They were angry, too, at the traders, who had siphoned off much of the cash due to the Indians from the sale of their lands and who continued to appropriate much — sometimes all — of the annuity payments owed to individuals. They resented the way they were treated by many whites and the abuse of Indian women. "Many of the whites always seemed to say by their manner when they saw an Indian, 'I am much better than you,' and the Indians did not like this. There was excuse for this, but the Dakota [Sioux] did not believe there were better men in the world than they."

Among the Sioux there was bitter division between those who favored the ways of the whites and those who clung to old values. Many of the latter blamed their chief, Little Crow, for the loss of their lands and scorned those "cut hairs" who had shorn their hair like whites and accepted government help to become farmers.

As the Civil War dragged into its second year, the Indians saw many white Minnesotans leave for military service. It was whispered among the Indians that the war was going badly for the North and that the South would win; now would be a good time to drive out the white settlers, they thought, and retrieve their lands before help could arrive.

Late on the night of August 17/18, 1862, Chief Little Crow was awakened with the news that four young braves, in an act of bravado, had killed five settlers at a farm, including two women. Because the Indians knew that the whites would exact disproportionate vengeance, they argued for an all-out, preemptive strike. Little Crow, aware of the overwhelming number of their antagonists, tried to dissuade them: "You may kill one — two — ten; yes, as many as the leaves in the forest yonder, and their brothers will not miss them. Kill one — two — ten, and ten times ten will come to kill you. Count your fingers all day long and white men with guns in their hands will come faster than you can count." In the end, while still convinced of the futility of the undertaking, Little Crow agreed to join his people in fighting the whites. "Taoyateduta [Little Crow] is not a coward," he said, "he will die with you."

Little Crow gave the order to attack the Agency that very morning. Groups of Indians dashed into the night to assault the settlers. The women made bullets; the men cleaned their guns. One of the first victims was a trader named Andrew

Myrick who, when the Indians had pleaded for food, told them they could eat grass. Now he lay dead on the ground, his mouth stuffed with grass. "Myrick is eating grass himself," said the Indians.

During the following days, the Sioux rampaged throughout the state, attacking outlying settlements, plundering, killing, and taking hundreds of women and children prisoner. In a plea to Washington to send aid, Minnesota governor Alexander Ramsey declared: "This is not our war; it is a national war."

After their initial successes things went badly for the Indians. Little Crow had trouble restraining the younger warriors, who were distracted by easy targets and thus gave the government soldiers time to organize effective resistance. The key to victory, the old warriors knew, was the capture of Fort Ridgely, which controlled the Minnesota Valley. Twice the Sioux attempted to take it by storm, but were thwarted by the army's artillery. The crucial defeat came on September 23, when a large force under General Henry H. Sibley successfully defended their stand at a place called Wood Lake. After this, Little Crow, along with the other leaders, Medicine Bottle and Little Six, fled westward with their bands to the open prairies and eventually to Canada. The fighting had lasted just under six weeks. About five hundred white settlers and soldiers had been killed during

the uprising and, while Indian casualties may have been less than a score, the ultimate price they paid was devastating.

About six hundred Indian men were captured, or persuaded to surrender on promise of leniency. The Military Commission set up to try them began its work on September 28. In a rush to dispose of the cases, as many as forty were heard in a single day; one trial lasted five minutes. By November 5, when it finished its work, the Commission had sentenced 307 prisoners to death. President Abraham

Medicine Bottle (Wa-Kan-O-Zhan-Zhan) awaiting execution while a prisoner at Fort Snelling, Minnesota, June 17, 1864. Albumen print by Joel Emmons Whitney.

Medicine Bottle, photographed here in a moment of despair, was one of the leaders of the uprising and took part in the unsuccessful attacks on Fort Ridgely. Having reached safety in Canada after the fighting, he and Little Six (Shakopee) were abducted by the American authorities, tried, and hanged.

Among the crowd of onlookers, several constables stand to attention as the lifeless bodies of Medicine Bottle and Little Six are framed against the fallen platform of the gallows. Their coffins lie ready for them below. While waiting to die, Little Six is reported to have heard the shriek of a train whistle in the distance and said: "As the white man comes in, the Indian goes out."

Lincoln called for a review of their perfunctory trials and revoked the death sentences of all but thirty-nine of the condemned. One of these was later reprieved. On the day after Christmas, 1862, the thirty-eight men were hanged together on a mass scaffold.

During the fighting, Governor Ramsey had declared: "The Sioux Indians of Minnesota must be exterminated or driven forever beyond the borders of the state." In the aftermath of the uprising, panic-stricken settlers made good this threat and called for the removal of all Native Americans from the state, ignoring the fact that many Sioux had refused to take part in the

fighting. About seventeen hundred Indians, mostly women and children, were confined near Fort Snelling; three hundred prisoners, including those whose sentences had been commuted, were still interned at Mankato. Not only the Sioux, but also the Winnebago Indians, who had played virtually no part in the war, were ultimately banished.

Many Indians died in captivity at Fort Snelling, during the harsh winter there. Those who survived were transported, in appalling conditions, on steamboats and in freight cars, to a desolate reservation in the Dakota Territory. When the operation was over, more than thirteen

Imprisoned Sioux near Fort Snelling,
Minnesota, 1862. Albumen print by
Benjamin Franklin Upton.
Separated from those charged directly
with the killing, a village of about
seventeen hundred Sioux, mostly
women and children, spent the winter
of 1862/63 under close guard on the
banks of the Minnesota River. The
image of a tipi village hemmed in by
stockade walls provided a fitting
metaphor of the Indians' future.

hundred Santee Sioux and nearly
two thousand Winnebago Indians
had been forcibly removed from the
state. The Sioux suffered three
years in their new location before
being moved to a Santee reservation
near Niobrara, Nebraska. Less than
two hundred of the so-called

"friendly" Sioux were allowed to
remain in Minnesota.

In June 1863, when the evacuation was nearing completion, Little
Crow returned to Minnesota with a
small group of Indians, hoping to
steal horses that would help them in
their life further west. While
picking raspberries with his son,
Little Crow was shot by two settlers, not because they recognized
him, but simply because he was an
Indian. His unidentified body was
brought to Hutchinson, scalped,
mutilated, and thrown on a slaugh-
terhouse waste heap. His identity
was confirmed only after his son
was captured nearly a month later.

The two men who had shot him received a $75 bounty on his scalp
and a $500 bonus for killing the
Sioux leader.

The two other leaders in the
uprising, Little Six and Medicine
Bottle, enjoyed their freedom only a
few months longer. In December a
U.S. Army Major, aided by an
American civilian, had them drugged
and spirited out of Canada to the
waiting authorities. Both were tried
by the military and hanged.

BITTER HARVEST

Just a few days prior to the uprising, photographer Adrian Ebell arrived at the Santee Reservation to photograph scenes of local life. He ignored the Indians encountered in traditional dress and face paint, and chose, instead, to photograph the "civilized" Sioux living at the Upper Agency, most of whom were farmers and some christianized. In his photograph of two women engaged in field work, an image that echoed the spirit of the French painter of peasant life, Jean-François Millet, Ebell projected a vision, shared by many whites, of an Indian world transformed by honest, hard work. Overlooked in this pleasant rural dream was the rage of a proud people dispossessed. The few Sioux in Minnesota who did give up their former lives for a brick house, land, oxen, and cash crops found themselves uneasily adrift between two mutually antagonistic worlds. Whites continued to view them with condescension, while many of their own people despised them for their apparent betrayal. This was demonstrated during the uprising when insurgents burned the houses of the "cut hairs," destroyed their fields, and, in some instances, forced them to exchange their white clothing for traditional dress and to join their war parties. The cultural turmoil caused by obstinate government policies of assimilation proved an enduring legacy.

Winnowing wheat, Upper Agency, Santee Sioux Reservation, Minnesota, August 1862. Albumen print by Adrian Ebell.

WARRIORS

I shall vanish and be no more,
But the land over which I now roam
Shall remain
And change not.

Omaha Warrior's Song

The names most cele-
brated in this period of
Indian history are those
of the great warrior
chiefs who led the fighting in defense of their home territories in the
Southwest and in the Great Plains.
They fought ancient tribal enemies
and the U.S. Army in battles that
exacted an almost unimaginable toll
of Native American lives. Tahirussa-
wichi, a Chaui Pawnee born about
1830, declared: "When I think of all
the people of my own tribe who have
died during my lifetime and then of
those in other tribes that have fallen
by our hands, they are so many that
they make a vast cover over Mother
Earth." Francis Parkman, who
had traveled the frontier in 1846,
returned there about 1870 and was
told that almost all members of a
band of Sioux with whom he had
lived had, in the interval, been
killed fighting the whites.

Among the Plains tribes, warfare was considered the natural fulfillment of life for most able-bodied
men. Warriors were first and fore-
most protectors of the tribe and of
the family, but warfare was also
pursued for its own sake, as the
principal field of honor on which
prestige and wealth were won.
Training began in childhood, when
games mimicked the skills that
would be called upon in adult life,
and fathers and uncles set up trials
to prepare the would-be warrior for
the hardships ahead. Ohiyesa, a
Santee Sioux who was four years old
at the time of the Minnesota Upris-

ing, told how his uncle would send
him to find water in strange country
in the middle of the night or startle
him awake in the morning with gun-
shots and fierce war whoops, to in-
still in him the resourcefulness and
reflexes that he might need one day.

A warrior's life began with a
"vision quest" in which fasting and
prayer revealed the individual spirit
forces, or medicine, that would
protect him. There were many other

rites and ceremonies associated
with war, designed to ensure and
celebrate victory, but also to express
a fatalistic recognition of death and
defeat. Among the Cheyennes and
Sioux, for example, the warrior's
preparation for battle was also a
preparation for death; for he put on
his war bonnet and finest clothing,
rebraided his hair, and painted his
face so as to present his best
appearance both to the enemy and

◁ *The Great Scalp Taker (Pa-Ha-Uza Tan-Ka), a Santee Sioux warrior, probably 1862. Albumen print by Joel Emmons Whitney.*
The sixteen feathers worn in the headdress were said to represent the number of scalps this warrior had taken.

△ *Northern Cheyenne warriors at Fort Keogh, 1889. Albumen print by Christian Barthelmess.*
The superb fighting skills of Indian warriors were acknowledged by all who encountered them. The U.S. Army knew the Indians not only as adversaries, but also as allied scouts and fighters who served with them in campaigns against mutual enemies. Here, a group of

warriors in native dress arrives at Fort Keogh, Montana, where, in accordance with the plans of Lieutenant E. W. Casey, they were to be the first Native Americans given the same disciplined training and uniforms as regular soldiers. This Cheyenne fighting unit, L Troop, Eighth Cavalry, later became known as "Casey's Scouts."

ciple of warfare by stating that his dual aim was "to kill the enemy and save our own men." The superb effectiveness of the Indians' hit-and-run tactics can be measured by a statement made by General William Tecumseh Sherman to the Secretary of War in 1867: "My opinion is if fifty Indians are allowed to remain between the Arkansas and Platte [rivers], we will have to guard every stage station, every train, and all railroad working parties. In other words, fifty hostile Indians will checkmate three thousand soldiers."

◁ *Gall (Pizi), Chief of the Hunkpapa Sioux, 1880s. Gelatin silver print by David F. Barry.*
An orphan who became Sitting Bull's adoptive brother, Gall was a leading war chief in the Sioux wars of the 1860s and 1870s. Along with Crazy Horse, of whom no reliable photographic record exists, he led the successful assault on General George Armstrong Custer and his troops at the Battle of the Little Bighorn on June 25, 1876.

Powder Face, Arapaho war chief, ▷
photographed at Camp Supply, Indian Territory, 1870. Original negative by William S. Soule.
The warrior's regalia includes feathered war bonnet, pipe-stem breastplate, and buckskin shirt fringed with scalplocks. The curved lance (Pa-bon), decorated with feathers and wrapped with fur, identifies him as leader of the Tonkonko, or Black Legs, one of six Kiowa warrior societies. By fixing this lance in the ground during battle and securing himself to it with a sash, its owner pledged never to retreat.

to the Great Spirit, should he come to meet the latter. An exception were those warriors who, after preparing themselves through prayer and ritual exercise, fought naked, their bodies painted to represent the special medicine that would give them power and protection in battle. Among the war songs that have been preserved are some of the most poignant expressions of the warrior's acceptance of his uncertain fate on earth. "Let us see, is this real/Let us see, is this real/This life I am living?" sang the Pawnee warrior in contemplating a mission

from which he was unlikely to return.

Although exhorted to courage in every way, Indian warriors found incomprehensible the kind of stand-up tactics adopted by white soldiers and the willingness of whites deliberately to sacrifice men in battle. Instead, the Indian mode of fighting was extremely attentive to human life, relying on surprise and elusiveness to conserve every man possible. This was both the wisdom and the necessity of survival in a finite society. The famous Sauk warrior Black Hawk expressed this prin-

Curly Chief or One Who Strikes the ▷
Chief First (Tectasakariku), Pawnee,
c. 1870. Albumen print by William
Henry Jackson.
Tectasakariku became chief of the
Kitkehahkis through his prowess as a
warrior. His head is shaved in
accordance with Pawnee custom, with
a long scalp lock at the crown that is
ornamented with a feather. He led
his band on its passage to a new reservation in Indian Territory in 1874.

The costumes and ceremonial
paraphernalia commonly associated
with Native Americans of all tribes
had in large part a military origin,
offering a record of battle honors
instantly comprehensible to the
onlooker. Achievements might be
indicated by the wearing of a
feathered war bonnet or by the way
head feathers were trimmed and
notched to specify particular deeds
or experiences, such as the taking of
a scalp or a wound suffered in
battle. For the Cheyennes, a war
bonnet served as recognition of the
warrior who had proved himself
through courage and experience in
battle. It was left up to the individual to decide if it was merited, although a warrior's peers might either
encourage the naturally modest or
shame the man who had presumed
to adopt it too soon. Honors gained
in life also accompanied a warrior
to his grave. In some tribes, great
chiefs were laid to rest, in a tipi,
dressed in their finest clothing, with
their weapons, favorite possessions,
and even their slain horses nearby.

Names were sometimes given
to warriors to reflect their fighting
prowess. Pawnee Killer, Plenty
Coups, One Who Strikes the Chief
First, He Kills First, and One Who
Catches the Enemy are examples.

Apart from individual achievements, memories of events of major
importance to the tribe could also
be kept alive over many years by
oral tradition. Pawnees around
1870 could repeat details, including
names of participants and battle
tactics, of the war between various
bands that had unified their nation
a century before.

However fearsome and lonely
the task might be, the warrior spirit
would surge to the fore, particularly

53

slowed his advance. When the Nez Perces were finally caught near the Canadian border, Looking Glass argued for continuing the fight, but was killed on the last day of the siege. The next day, Chief Joseph delivered his famous surrender speech, which concluded with the words: "Hear me, my chiefs, I am tired; my heart is sick and sad. From where the sun now stands I will fight no more forever."

Quanah Parker, a Comanche warrior, c. 1890. Albumen print, possibly by Hutchins, Hutchins & Lenny. ▷
Son of a Comanche chief and a white taken captive as a child, Quanah became a leader in the Comanche Wars of the 1860s and 1870s. Refusing to be a party to the 1867 Medicine Lodge Treaty that assigned reservation lands to the Comanches, Kiowas, Apaches, Cheyennes, and Arapahos, he fought relentlessly against intruders on Comanche territories. In 1871 he re-pelled the incursion of Colonel Ranald S. Mackenzie's forces onto the Staked Plains of Texas and, when commercial buffalo hunters arrived there three years later, he personally led a joint force of seven hundred Comanche, Kiowa, Cheyenne, and Arapaho warriors in an unsuccessful attack on the hunters' stronghold at Adobe Walls. He was forced to surrender after troops led by Colonel Nelson A. Miles captured and destroyed the militant's herd of horses and tipis at Palo Duro Canyon in 1874.

Looking Glass (Allalimya Takanin), of the Nez Perces, mounted on a painted war pony, 1871. Albumen print by William Henry Jackson.

An attack on his peaceful village by General Oliver Otis Howard's troops led Looking Glass to join the Nez Perces under Chief Joseph on their thirteen hundred-mile flight toward freedom in the summer and autumn of 1877. Looking Glass became their principal war chief, but, believing that he had eluded his pursuers, left the camp open to a surprise attack at Big Hole, Montana, and was later replaced. He led a war party that stampeded Howard's pack train and considerably

among the younger braves, who were eager for excitement and anxious to prove themselves in the world. The human cost is nowhere better revealed than in an account by the Sioux Ohiyesa who, as a boy around 1870 or 1872, witnessed the departure of a small, youthful war party after a favorable omen had been received from the medicine man: "Our young men presently received their sign, and for a few days all was hurry and excitement. On the appointed morning we heard the songs of the warriors and the wailing of the women, by which they bade adieu to each other, and the eligible braves, headed by an experienced man — old Hotanka or Loud-Voiced Raven — set out for Gros Ventre country. . . . From the early morning when these braves left us, led by the old war priest . . . the anxious mothers, sisters and sweethearts counted the days. Old Smoky Day would occasionally get up early in the morning, and sing a 'strong-heart' song for his absent grandson. I still seem to hear the hoarse, cracked voice of the ancient singer as it resounded among the woods. For a long time our roving community enjoyed unbroken peace, and we were spared any trouble or disturbance. Our hunters often brought in a deer or elk or bear for fresh meat. The beautiful lakes furnished us with fish and wild-fowl for variety. The placid waters, as the autumn advanced, reflected the variegated colors of the changing foliage . . . . One frosty morning — for it was then near the end of October — the weird song of a solitary brave was heard. In an instant the camp was thrown into indescribable confusion. The meaning of this was clear as day to everybody — all of our war-party were killed, save the one whose mournful song announced the fate of his companions. The lonely warrior was Bald Eagle.

"The village was convulsed with grief; for in sorrow as in joy, every Indian shares with all the others. The old women stood still, wherever they might be, and wailed dismally, at intervals chanting the praises of the departed warriors. The wives went a little way from their tepees and there audibly mourned; but the young maidens wandered further away from the camp, where no one could witness their grief. The old men joined in the crying and singing. To all appearances the most unmoved of all were the warriors, whose tears must be poured forth in the country of the enemy to embitter their vengeance. They sat silently within their lodges, and strove to conceal their feelings behind a stoical countenance."

A VICTIM IN KANSAS

The mutilated body of Sergeant Frederick Wylyams, killed on June 26, 1867. Albumen print by Dr. William Abraham Bell.

The photographer recorded this gruesome scene near Fort Wallace, Kansas, while working for the Kansas Pacific Survey. The victim, an English recruit serving with the 7th Cavalry, was killed in a fight with a group of Cheyenne Indians, who stripped and mutilated his body. When found, he had been scalped, his throat was cut, his torso and thighs deeply slashed, and the tissue torn from the lower right arm. A wound at the chest laid bare his heart. The corpse was finally shot through with arrows. For the Indians it was the ultimate indignity to send an enemy thus broken and disfigured into the afterlife. Bell, trained as a doctor, recorded the scene with an unblinking, clinical eye, and sent off copies of the picture to Washington so that, in his words, "the authorities should see how their soldiers were treated on the Plains." A U.S. Army officer who witnessed the scene put it less decorously when, alluding to the current mood of official tolerance toward Native Americans, he said the purpose was "just to show our friends at Washington, the Indian Agents, what fiends we have to deal with!" Only after more than a decade of further carnage were any comparable photographs of Indian casualties circulated.

CHRONICLES OF WAR:
A PAWNEE BUFFALO ROBE

*Buffalo robe painted with battle
scenes, probably 1871. Albumen print
by William Henry Jackson. Details
opposite.*

Indian history and lore was largely passed down by word of mouth from generation to generation. Exceptional events in the life of the tribe or of individuals were sometimes documented in pictographs, as with this painted buffalo robe, which the frontier photographer William Henry Jackson went to the unusual trouble of photographing. In addition to depicting details of group battles, such robes were often painted with scenes of individual war exploits.

An early traveler in the West told how, when an army officer in council with the Pawnees once urged the tribe to live in peace, a brave named Wild Warrior rose to speak. His buckskin shirt and leggings were fringed with enemy scalps; other scalps were fashioned into a wig that he had set upon his shaved head. On his back was a painted battle robe, and his reply provided a vivid indication of what such personal records could mean: "the Sioux came down upon us and murdered our fathers, our mothers, our wives and our little ones; and the lodges in which they dwelt were burned to the ground.... *I* could not agree to [peace] while my people's bones lay unburned and unrevenged. I thirsted for the blood of my enemies. Alone I pursued them—I followed them through heat and through cold—through storm and sunshine, and when hungering; still, still I followed them! One by one they felt the edge of my tomahawk, until all there fell. I have revenged my people. Others may be advised to peace, but I was born to

slay my enemies. Wa-con-dah [Great Spirit] made me a great warrior. He decreed that I should be successful in procuring furs for my white brethren, and scalps for my self, and I have

done so." Spreading out his battle robe, Wild Warrior presented it to the officer, saying: "Take it to your home, that your people may know of [my] deeds!"

PLAINS HUNTERS

*Make the buffalo come near and the clouds
and wind fair to approach them, that we may always
have meat in camp to feed us and you.
Help us in every way;
let our children live. Let us live. Call on all these spirits
and ask them to assist you in helping us.*

From a prayer to departed relatives (Assiniboine)

The buffalo and the horse were defining elements in the culture of the North American Plains Indians. For centuries they had existed as nomadic hunters, following the great herds of buffalo on their annual migrations and depending on them for virtually every necessity of life. With their survival at stake, the Plains Indians fiercely defended their hunting territories.

The use of horses, a legacy of the early Spanish settlers in Mexico, was almost universal among Native Americans in the eighteenth century. The horse revolutionized the lives of the ancient Plains dwellers, greatly expanding their range of travel and making possible the transport of the large, heavy tipis that became the trademark of their culture. As the object on which both hunting and warfare depended, horses became the principal measure of wealth, used for dowries, presents, and barter. Horse-stealing raids became a regular part of Plains military life.

Horses transformed the nature of buffalo hunting, and the mounted chase evolved into a breathtaking performance of riding skills and marksmanship. Racing over the open plains at full speed,

---

Mountain buffalo, 1880s. Albumen print by an unknown photographer.

the riders closed on their giant quarry, clinging to their mounts with their legs only, as they wielded bow and arrows or firearms with deadly accuracy. The photographer Solomon Carvalho witnessed a hunt in which a Delaware Indian, riding furiously, repeatedly rested his rifle on the saddle while balancing himself on one leg; the other leg he threw over the rifle to steady it. Then, leaning to one side to be level with the gun, he quickly took aim and fired, rarely missing his mark.

The entire tribe participated in major annual buffalo hunts, and strict discipline was maintained to ensure that lone hunters would not frighten the animals too soon. The division of the spoils was similarly well regulated. To the man who killed an animal went the skin and the choicest cuts of meat; the other parts were distributed in order of family and tribal standing. Even the poorest members of the tribe were assured of something. A successful hunt was followed by days of feasting on fresh meat. The surplus was cut into strips or sheets and hung on wooden poles to dry, providing a store of food for leaner days.

In addition to food, the buffalo provided most other necessities of life. Hides yielded leather for clothing, storage bags, shields, ropes, and tipi coverings. Buffalo robes, made from whole hides with the fur still attached, served as outer garments in cold weather and as blankets and mattresses. From the

Arapaho camp, c. 1870. Albumen print by William S. Soule.

The family members, including one child, seen in front of their leather tipi are not identified. The subjects watched the photographer as carefully as he them, with feelings that seem to range from suspicion to mild amusement. Looking at the arms in the group at left reveals that a further figure hid his or her face from the camera. Some details of tipi construction are unusually clear, including the seams between individual hides, the wooden pegs used to join the covering at the front, and the entrance flap made from a hide with its fur still attached. In the background stands a rack with slabs of drying meat and, on the ground, a hide staked out for tanning.

animal's sinew came string for bows and thread for sewing and making rope. The stomach was a ready-made vessel for carrying water or for storing fat and marrow. Buffalo horns were fashioned into spoons, cups, and other utensils.

The main hunt took place in the summer months, when the animals were fat and their coats thinned out, making for easier dressing. Buffalo killed in winter, when their coats were thick, provided the most desirable material for bedding and robes. The finest buffalo hide robe was considered to be that made from a heifer killed in autumn. Many other varieties of game, including birds, deer, elk, and antelope, were hunted for food and clothing, the finest garments being those fashioned from deer or elk skin.

The need for frequent moves in search of game was facilitated by the ingenious Plains tipi, a portable dwelling of sewn buffalo hides stretched over a conical framework of slender poles. Depending on the tribe, three or four base poles were

◁ *Southern Cheyenne village, Wyoming, c. 1880. Albumen print by Charles W. Carter.*

Some seventy-five tipis appear in this view, with others undoubtedly out of sight; this suggests a village of five to six hundred people. In the left foreground a woman, barely discernible, works on a buffalo hide hanging between a tree and a pole. In the middle distance a group of four of five figures, silhouetted against a tipi, prepare a hide staked out on the ground. At center right is a tipi painted with Maltese crosses, symbols of the Morning Star; another like it is partly visible at the edge of the frame. In front of the painted tipi are others with travois poles and several wickerwork baskets before them. These were used to carry children or fragile objects while traveling.

Piegan (Blackfoot) Indians arriving at Fort Macleod, Alberta, Canada, 1882. Albumen print by Daniel Cadzo.
Outfitted for travel, the group includes many saddled mounts. Other horses are equipped with travois stacked with bundles.   ▽

first raised to serve as a foundation, with the rest of the poles — usually from ten to twenty — added to complete the frame. The hide covering was wrapped around it and secured in front and on the ground by wooden pegs. An opening left at the top allowed smoke from the fires to escape and was regulated by side flaps to allow for shifts in wind or for rain. Over time, the rising smoke gradually blackened the peaks of the otherwise whitish tents. Exposure to the

elements and constant wear meant that the tipi covers needed to be replaced periodically. A large tipi might rise to a height of twenty-five feet, and its covering of fifteen to eighteen hides weigh several hundred pounds.

The tipi was a versatile shelter, whose configuration changed with the seasons. In winter, when the rhythm of life slowed and people left the open plain for campsites in sheltered valleys, the tipi's entrance would be shut tight and the interior fitted with a lining, while snow or brush was banked on the outside to keep out the drafts. In summer the bottom edges were often rolled up or a whole side left open to admit the cooling breeze.

Sioux ceremonial dance, Pine Ridge, South Dakota, 1880s. Albumen print by an unknown photographer.
Religious and ceremonial dances accompanied by drums, rattles, and other instruments were held for many purposes, but especially in connection with warfare and hunting. With their throbbing rhythms, piercing whoops, and often ecstatic emotional states, dances were a part of Native American ritual life that often both fascinated and unnerved white observers, who frequently misunderstood their purpose. The most important of the Plains rituals was the Sun Dance, performed by men in fulfillment of a vow after victory in battle, recovery from sickness, or some other form of deliverance. It was accompanied by fasting and acts of self-torture. The dance performed by this group has not been identified.

TANNING BUFFALO HIDES

During a visit to a Cheyenne village at the mouth of the Yellowstone River around 1870, Stanley J. Morrow recorded, in a unique series of images, the traditional stages in preparing and using buffalo hides. This work, assigned to women, involved much patience and hard labor, since a green hide from a large buffalo might weigh fifty pounds and take ten days or more to treat properly. After a successful hunt, the hides were stripped from the animals in the field and then brought to camp for curing. Fresh hides were staked to the ground or, in some cases, stretched on a wooden frame. With a scraper typically made of elk antler, remnants of flesh and fat were removed and the hide scraped to an even thickness. Scraping was repeated on the outer side to remove the hair, and then the hide was allowed to dry in the sun. At this stage the uncured leather was known as rawhide—an extremely tough material used for carrying cases called parfleches, for shields, drumheads, thongs, and other items of everyday use that needed to be extremely durable. For tanned leather a compound of the animal's brains, fat, and liver was rubbed into the hide, a process that was repeated several times as it dried in the sun. After wetting with water, the hide was rolled up and allowed to dry and shrink. It was then stretched, scraped clean, and finally softened by drawing it back and

*Stretching hides for a tipi, c. 1870.
Frame from an albumen stereograph by
Stanley J. Morrow.*
The woman standing at left is
softening a hide by drawing it back and
forth around a cord tied to the pole.
The other uses a bone scraper on an
unfinished hide.

forth around an animal skin cord tied to a pole. Smoking the leather would ensure that it did not stiffen after getting wet. Much buffalo leather was employed for tipi coverings, but it was also used for moccasins and robes. Although buffalo hide was too coarse to make ideal clothing—for this the skins of other animals were preferred— old leather from a worn-out tipi is known to have sometimes been recycled into children's clothing.

Making a tipi cover, c. 1870.
Frame from an albumen stereograph by
Stanley J. Morrow.
Two women cut and piece together tanned hides that have been stripped o hair. A curved knife used for trimming lies in the foreground. Behind the women are racks of drying buffalo meat.

◁ *Scraping hides, c. 1870.*
Frame from an albumen stereograph by
Stanley J. Morrow.
Two women bend over a buffalo hide staked out on the ground, scraping away its fleshy side. About ten such hides are visible in the photograph. The iron pot at left may have contained the ingredients for tanning.

When it was time to move on, the tipi covering was folded and placed on a horse travois, a carrier made by fastening two long poles at the withers of a horse and allowing them to drag behind. Those who witnessed it never ceased to marvel at the spectacle of many hundreds of people on the move, men, women, and children, with loaded horses and mules, innumerable dogs, and mounted warriors riding alongside, their weapons at the ready. The job of moving camp was assigned to the women, who dismantled and set up the tipis and afterward attended to other heavy domestic chores, such as gathering wood, hauling water, cooking, making clothes, and dressing animal skins. The activities of the men were confined almost exclusively to hunting and warfare.

A proper campsite required a supply of water, wood for fire (or dried buffalo dung as a substitute), and forage for horses. The dependence on nearby resources imposed a natural limit on the size of any Plains community, governed the length of its stay at a given site, and made it especially vulnerable to destructive enemy raids. At the best of times, life in the wild for these nomadic hunters could be idyllic, but theirs was a precarious existence in which hunger and sudden dangers were never far off. This was demonstrated in 1869 when the photographer Stanley Morrow described a disaster in Montana that recently had befallen a band of Yankton Sioux led by Two Bear. While camped peacefully on the Knife River, the tribe had smelled smoke, but, as the air was still, could not identify its source. About midnight a breeze sprang up and drove a wildfire directly into their sleeping camp, burning up sixty tipis and many horses, killing nine people, and inflicting horrible burns on many others, including numerous children.

By the 1880s, with the great buffalo herds all but vanished and many Indian tribes confined to

Winter in Spotted Eagle's village, 1879. Frame from an original stereograph negative by Laton Alton Huffman.
A thin crust of snow covers the ground in front of the light-colored tipi belonging to Spotted Eagle. The tree stump was one of many left by Indians in need of fuel. To the right, next to a large pile of split wood, stands a buffalo hide stretched on a frame; further hides are stacked against Spotted Eagle's tipi.

reservations, the traditional tipi village was becoming increasingly rare; canvas now replaced leather as the covering material. The village of Chief Spotted Eagle, who surrendered with his band of nearly 2,500 Sioux near Fort Keogh, Montana, in 1879, was said to be the last great leather lodge village seen on the Yellowstone River. The experienced Indian fighter, General Nelson A. Miles, said of it: "This was the last place, so far as I know, where the Indian still used buffalo meat for his food, tanned the skins for his leather lodge, and the robes for his blanket." The photographer L. A. Huffman noted that Spotted Eagle's people were very poor, and that one could see where hungry dogs had chewed holes in the tipis at night in order to get at the sinews with which the pieces of hide were sewn together. These holes had to be patched up with cloth.

Cheyenne medicine lodge on the Yellowstone River, 1870s. Frame from an albumen stereograph by Stanley J. Morrow.
Attached to the very top of this tribal medicine lodge is a crescent-shaped medicine bundle fringed with hair; other bundles hung over the entrance. Such bundles contained various sacred objects linked to the welfare of the tribe. The images on the tipi covering — a spotted buffalo head with a serpentine body, and another type of buffalo head to the left — allude to the magic powers possessed by the owners.

Arapaho camp near the Canadian River, Oklahoma, 1869. Albumen print by William S. Soule.

COUNCIL AT FORT LARAMIE, 1868

In 1868 men came out and brought papers. We are ignorant and do not read papers, and they did not tell us right what was in these papers. We wanted them to take away their forts, leave our country, would not make war, and give our traders something. They said we had bound ourselves to trade on the Missouri, and we said, no, we did not want that. The interpreters deceived us.

Chief Red Cloud, July 16, 1870

In the spring of 1868 representatives of several powerful Plains tribes, including the Oglala, Brule, Miniconjou Sioux, Northern Cheyenne, Crow, and Arapaho, gathered at Fort Laramie, Wyoming, to meet members of a U.S. Peace Commission who were attempting to put an end to the bitter fighting — later known as Red Cloud's War — in the Powder River country. Two years earlier, the authorities had met the Sioux to negotiate a treaty allowing safe passage for travelers and the building of new forts (named for C. F. Smith and Phil Kearny) along the route leading from Fort Laramie to the mining town of Bozeman, Montana. However, when seven hundred soldiers, led by Colonel Henry B. Carrington, arrived during the council — thereby demonstrating that the military had already decided to build the forts — a sub-chief of the Oglala Sioux named Red Cloud angrily left with his followers, vowing never to yield the country and his hunting lands to

All photographs in this section were taken by Alexander Gardner at Fort Laramie in 1868. Those on pages 76, 77, 79, 82, and 83 are frames from albumen stereographs, the others large-format albumen prints. The stereos are reproduced from the only set known to exist.

Group of Cheyenne chiefs.
Only the man at right was identified by Gardner. He is Little Wolf, leading chief of the Cheyennes, who would later continue to fight alongside Crazy Horse and, in 1877, gave himself up with the latter. After seeing many of his people die on an alien reservation assigned to them in Indian Territory, Little Wolf led his people in a dramatic escape back to their homeland. Battles with U.S. Army troops nearly wiped out his Northern Cheyenne tribe. The other men in the photograph may be Dull Knife (center), who joined Little Wolf on the flight northward, and Short Hair (left), a chief who was mentally deranged. His cropped and disheveled hair suggests that he may have been in mourning.

Interior of the council chamber; Man Afraid of His Horses (Tasunkakokipapi) smoking the sacred pipe. ▷
More than a social formality, the smoking of a pipe had a sacred character, playing an important part in councils and other solemn occasions. Smoking under such circumstances was considered an act of supplication to spirits to bring good fortune and assistance. It was an ancient practice virtually universal among Native Americans. The pipe itself was often a venerated object, held in safekeeping by chosen officials.

white intruders. Although the forts were built, Red Cloud and his warriors kept the area in a constant state of warfare for two years. The photographer Ridgway Glover was an incidental casualty of this bloody campaign, and eighty men under Captain William J. Fetterman were killed in December 1866 in the ambush known as the Fetterman Massacre, one of the major events in the annals of American Indian warfare.

The eight-man Peace Commission dispatched by the government in 1868 had an equal number of civilian and military members. One of the former, Nathaniel G. Taylor, was in charge. Once a Methodist minister, and now Commissioner of Indian Affairs, Taylor led the efforts toward what he believed was humanitarian treatment of the Indians. Earlier he had catalogued the injustices done to the Indian and warned of the escalation of a con-

flict that was already costing the government one million dollars a week: "If we want the war we have provoked enlarged and intensified till our whole frontier is in a blaze, till our infant Territories are isolated and besieged and Pacific overland communications cut off, we have only to press a little further the policy we are now pursuing and we will get all we desire." The chief military representative on the Commission was General William

◁ Fire Thunder, Man Afraid of His Horses, and Pipe.

Scene at a Crow camp. ▽
The central figure appears to be
attending to a large cut of meat, while
the one at left seems startled by the
photographer's arrival.

Tecumseh Sherman, Commander of the Department of the Missouri. Sherman had become famous for his relentless, punishing tactics during the Civil War, and events would prove his approach to fighting Indians to be no less harsh. In the present climate of conciliation toward the Indians, Sherman was forced to bide his time.

Among those present at the meetings was Alexander Gardner, who acted as the government's official photographer. He arrived at Fort Laramie at the end of April in the company of General Sherman, by which time a treaty had already been signed with the Brule Sioux. Other tribes reached Fort Laramie over the next several weeks. Delegations of Crows, Northern Cheyennes, and Northern Arapahos arrived a few days after Gardner and met the Commissioners in early May.

The treaty being offered the Indians was the standard one, pro-

Group of council chiefs; from left to right: Spotted Tail, Roman Nose, Man Afraid of His Horses, Lone Horn, Whistling Elk, Pipe, Slow Bull.
Of the leaders pictured, the Southern Cheyenne chief Roman Nose was the most celebrated warrior, possessed of medicine, it was believed, that protected him from the whites' bullets. In September 1868, knowing that its power had been inadvertently broken, he nevertheless led the charge in the Battle of Beecher's Island and was killed.

viding for an end to hostilities, the establishment of tribal boundaries, provision for food, health care, and other benefits, and eventual land grants to individuals. The Commission was also authorized to concede to Red Cloud the closing of the Bozeman Trail and the dismantling of the forts that had provoked the fighting.

Gardner photographed the meetings between the Peace Commissioners and representatives of various tribes, the distribution of gifts to the Indians, and views of the fort and surrounding countryside. Some of his most interesting work, however, consisted of informal scenes of everyday camp life among the Indians. In several of his photographs Gardner took advantage of the stereo camera's facility for taking "instantaneous" views and, in catching his subjects off guard, produced snapshots that showed them in their natural attitudes, not posed for the camera. Also remarkable was his interest in a wide spectrum of Indian people, from stalwart chiefs to old women and little children. He was one of the few photographers to pursue his subjects in intimate, private settings and, in several images, managed to capture a simple moment of laughter among people who, though usually impassive in the presence of whites, were among themselves fond of storytelling and humor. It was a measure of the times that many of the Indians photographed by

Gardner had their hair cut short in mourning.

The climax of the meetings occurred with the arrival, on May 21, of a band of northern Oglala Sioux led by Man Afraid of His Horses, a respected chief and Red Cloud's personal representative. He informed the Commissioners that Red Cloud refused to come to the council until the army had actually abandoned their forts along the Powder River. The Commissioners met the Oglalas in council on May 24 and 25 in four tipis set up together. Man Afraid of His Horses

Arapaho children.
The girl at center carries an infant on her back and, like the boy standing beside her, wears fine ornamented leggings beneath the plain, tattered overgarment.

Crow woman cooking.   ▷
Smoke from a fire obscures the lower part of the photograph. The woman wears a buffalo robe and has her hair cut short in mourning.

was photographed listening to the proceedings and smoking his ceremonial pipe. On May 25 he was informed that the forts would be removed. A few days later, the Miniconjous arrived, led by Lone Horn, who met the Commissioners on May 28. The Indians were pleased by the concession won from the military, but some remained skeptical. The Oglala chief, Four Bears, stated: "You say that you will protect us for thirty years, but I do not believe it." It was clear from what the Indians said, however, that they did not understand the boundaries of the reservation fixed by the treaty.

Red Cloud never attended the meetings, but a copy of the treaty was left at the fort for him to sign. The Commissioners then moved on for councils elsewhere. At the end of July the military abandoned the Powder River forts. From the hills Red Cloud and his men watched the troops march out, then came down and burned the forts to the ground. In November, Red Cloud arrived at Fort Laramie with a large contingent of Oglalas and Brules and signed the treaty as evidence of his good faith. It was a stunning victory for Red Cloud and his followers to have forced the withdrawal of the army from tribal lands, yet their success was marred by the evident confusion as to the terms of the treaty itself.

A far-reaching outcome of the Commission's proceedings was the recommendation that the government cease treating Native American tribes in the special category of "domestic dependent nations" and deal with them instead as individuals subject to United States laws, thereby obliterating Indian national or political identity. In March 1871 Congress passed a statute upholding existing treaties, but stating: "That hereafter no Indian nation or tribe within the territory of the United States shall be acknowledged or recognized as an independent nation, tribe, or power with whom the United States may contract by treaty."

Sioux warrior with mare and colt. The warrior wears one of the Confederate coats given as presents to some Indians attending the council. Like several others there, he wears an ornament highly prized by warriors: a pendant of metal discs attached to his braided scalp lock. It was long enough to reach the ground when the wearer was mounted on a horse.

RED CLOUD

The real victor of the Fort Laramie council was the man who refused to take part. A celebrated warrior, with eighty coups to his credit, Red Cloud led the opposition to white encroachment upon the Dakota lands. It was said that he could put three thousand warriors in the field, and among those who fought alongside him were some of the most famous of Plains fighters, including Crazy Horse, Roman Nose, Dull Knife, Little Wolf, Hump, Gall, and Rain In The Face. In the Powder River War their hit-and-run tactics and constant harassment of U.S. Army troops succeeded in pinning down the soldiers in the forts, forcing them to travel only with a heavy escort.

In later years Red Cloud fell out with some of his former allies over his decision—which he took under pressure—to cede the Black Hills. He remained, nonetheless, one of the most respected and able leaders in subsequent decades.

After some of Red Cloud's followers, and his son, took part in the Battle of the Little Bighorn in June 1876, the U.S. authorities accused Red Cloud himself of aiding the fighters and replaced him as principal chief by Spotted Tail.

Red Cloud (Mahpiuha Luta), Chief of the Oglala Sioux, 1876. Albumen print by Stanley J. Morrow.

This early portrait was taken on December 8, 1876, at the Red Cloud agency in Nebraska, a few months after he had been deposed as chief. Contrary to Morrow's belief, his was not the first photograph of Red Cloud, who had sat for his portrait once before, on a visit to Washington.

PAWNEE VILLAGE

*It is too soon to send missionaries among us.
We are not starving yet. We wish to enjoy hunting
until the wild animals are extinct. Let us use up
the wild animals before you make us work and spoil
our happiness.*

Pawnee chief, 1821

William H. Jackson took this series of pictures of a Pawnee village while returning from the Yellowstone Valley, where he had served as photographer to the expedition led by Dr. Ferdinand Vandiveer Hayden. The tribe's last northern settlement, it was located on the Loup River, a northward tributary of the Platte River in eastern Nebraska about one hundred miles west of Omaha and Council Bluffs.

Historically, the Pawnee had ranked among the most powerful of Plains tribes. They were renowned fighters whose war parties set out from their home in central Nebraska to roam as far south as New Mexico and northern Texas. During the Indian wars of the 1860s and 1870s, Pawnee warriors served as fighting scouts for the U.S. Army in campaigns against the traditional Pawnee enemy, the Sioux, and the latter's Cheyenne and Arapaho allies. Although still energetic as hunters and fighters, their years of greatness had passed when Jackson came across them. Beginning in 1833, when the Pawnee ceded all their lands south of the Platte River, their territory had been systematic-

All photographs in this section were taken by William Henry Jackson near Beaver Creek and Loup River in September 1871. Albumen prints.

Knee Mark on Ground When Stooping to Drink (Pahukatawa).
The chief of the Skidari clan of Skidi Pawnees is seated at the entrance to an earthlodge. He wears a feathered war bonnet with buffalo horns and ermine tassles; his lower body is wrapped in an ornamented buffalo robe. Suspended from his neck are two peace medals.

Sun Chief (Sukuru Lashar). ▷
According to the photographer, this depicts the successor to Pitalesharo, chief of the Chaui (Grand) Pawnee. The buffalo robe ornamented with stars and a crescent moon reflects Pawnee star worship. In their mythology, the Morning Star and the Evening Star, aided by the sun and the moon, gave life to the Pawnee people. On the warrior's chest is a James Buchanan Peace Medal of 1857.

ally diminished by treaty and their population decimated by disease and warfare. Between ten and twelve thousand Pawnee lived in Nebraska in the 1830s; by 1871, when these photographs were taken, they numbered only 2,364. All four bands of the Pawnee confederation — Skidis, Chauis (Grand), Kitkehahkis, and Pitahauerats — had been reduced to living in this single village, struggling not only to maintain their traditional ways, but literally to survive as a nation.

The Pawnee were both farmers and buffalo hunters. Their villages of solidly built earthlodges were used only part of the year. In the spring they planted crops of corn, squash, and beans. In late May or early June, as the plants started to develop, they left to wander across the prairies in search of buffalo, leaving the crops to grow unattended. During their hunts, which might involve journeys of eight or nine hundred miles, the Pawnee traveled like other Plains tribes and lived in tipis. In late summer they returned to their village to harvest their crops, much of which they dried and stored in deep underground caches for future use. In October they left once more to hunt buffalo, staying away during the coldest winter months and returning in spring to renew the annual cycle.

The Pawnee earthlodges were round, domed structures sunk partly below ground level and entered through a long, covered passageway. They were supported by a framework of stout wooden posts, an outer ring forming the perimeter wall and an inner ring of taller timbers providing the center support. An opening in the center of the roof admitted light and allowed smoke from the fire to escape. Beams supporting the roof were overlain with sticks and brush, and then sods or earth, to form a dense, insulating layer. The floors of the lodges were of tamped earth. In the center was a fire pit and, at the back wall, opposite the entrance, a raised altar platform. Each lodge could hold several families, with the interior partitioned by screens made

---

Pawnee earthlodges with a ceremonial gathering.
It has been conjectured that the ceremony taking place in the distance is that of a warrior's naming.

Children at the entrance to an earth-lodge.

The group of youngsters with a woman carrying a papoose may have been observing the ceremony shown in the view on the page opposite. The traditional treatment of the center boy's hair, with the head shaved except for a central ridge ending in a long scalp lock, was an aspect of Pawnee culture that Quaker authorities were eager to eradicate. Both he and the boy seated next to him have their ears pierced for earrings.

of reeds or skins. The lodges were large enough for favorite horses to be kept in a corner corral.

Great ceremony accompanied the laying of the ground plan and raising of an earth lodge, a task in which both men and women participated. In ancient times, according to their mythology, the Pawnee had been taught to build such dwellings by animals, badgers digging the holes for posts, beavers cutting, and bears carrying, the logs, and so forth. The four central posts of the lodge, each painted in symbolic colors, represented the central stars prominent in Pawnee religion: the Morning and Evening, and the North and South stars. Pawnee society was characterized by priesthoods and secret associations, with shrines playing an important part in an elaborate religious system that entailed the observation of many rituals and ceremonies. Until the early nineteenth century they had

been one of the few tribes to practice human sacrifice, offering a female captive each year to the Morning Star.

By the 1870s the Pawnee were getting the worst of both worlds, supplanted in the south and east by white settlers and menaced in the north and west by their Sioux enemies. In part because of their friendship with whites, the Pawnee became a prime objective of reformers wanting to raise them up to "civilization." The U.S. government sought to break up the village organization and undermine the

authority of traditional chiefs. On one occasion, in 1862, schoolchildren were forcibly separated from their families as they left for the buffalo hunt, the boys made to cut off their scalp locks, wear hats (which they detested), and toil in the fields — which the Pawnee considered to be women's work, demeaning to a warrior. When one boy was removed from the Agency school by his parents the following year, the school head asked the Indian agent to rule that children once placed in school became the property of the government.

The large Sioux presence in the heart of their buffalo hunting grounds restricted and threatened the Pawnee hunts. At the same time, their fixed villages made them easy targets for the Sioux raiding parties that regularly assailed them, killing both women working in the fields and their warrior defenders. In 1860 the Sioux, Cheyennes, and Arapahos raided the Loup River Pawnee villages once or twice a month. The government, which had promised to help defend the villages, was unable or unwilling to do so. A sod wall was erected around the village for protection, but did not stop the attacks. Sioux destroyed a Pawnee hunting party in the summer of 1873, killing a hundred or more people and taking great quantities of equipment and the meat and hides from eight hundred recently slaughtered buffalo. The outcome of this demoralizing defeat was a bitter division between those Pawnee who, with official encouragement, wished to escape their troubles by moving to a new reservation in Indian Territory, and those who desired to remain in their ancient homeland. In the end, pressure from the government overcame the opposition and, in 1874, the tribe forever left its village on the Loup River and was escorted south.

Warriors and children at the entrance to an earthlodge.
The warrior with an eagle feather in his hair is wrapped in a trade blanket and wears a hair-pipe breastplate; his companion carries a Long Knife, an army saber probably received as a present. Stacked across the entrance to the earthlodge are the long poles used in the construction of tipis during the biannual hunting expeditions. Puddles of water indicate the onset of the rainy season.

THE MANDANS

Like the Pawnee, a number of Plains tribes lived in earthlodge villages, including the Mandan, Arikara, Hidatsa, and, further eastward, the Omaha, Ponca, and Oto. Of these the Mandans were perhaps the best known, owing to the work of George Catlin, an artist and writer who lived among them in the 1830s and chronicled their lives. They were once a hardy and populous tribe, inhabiting at least nine villages on the Missouri River that served as trading centers. Catlin found the Mandans already weakened, hard-pressed by Sioux depredations and, he believed, poised on the edge of extinction. In the end, it was the white man's disease, against which Native Americans had little resistance, that proved more devastating than warfare. In 1837 an epidemic of smallpox raged in the upper Missouri region and left no more than 125 to 150 members of the tribe alive. Their chief, Four Bears (Mato-Tope), a victim of the disfiguring disease, reflected bitterly on this legacy of white "civilization":

Mandan village, Fort Berthold, North Dakota, 1870. Frame from an albumen stereograph by Stanley J. Morrow.
In a view almost hidden by a veritable forest of wooden racks for drying buffalo meat, one finds western-style log cabins alongside the Indians' traditional round earthlodges.

"I do not fear death," he said, "but to die with my face rotten, that even the wolves will shrink . . . at seeing me, and say to themselves, that is Four Bears, the friend of the whites." Along with remnants of the Arikaras and Hidatsas, who also had been decimated, the Mandan formed a village of two to three hundred lodges near Fort Berthold, a former fur trading post.

First and second Mandan chiefs, 1870. ▷
Frame from an albumen stereograph by Stanley J. Morrow.
The subjects were apparently photographed on the occasion of a peace treaty concluded between the Sioux, led by Two Bear, and the Mandan, Arikara, and Hidatsa tribes.

PUEBLOS

O our mother the Earth, O our Father the Sky,
Your children are we, and with tired backs
We bring you the gifts you love.
Then weave for us a garment of brightness;
May the warp be the white light of morning,
May the weft be the red light of evening,
May the fringes be the falling rain,
May the border be the standing rainbow.
Thus weave for us a garment of brightness,
That we may walk fittingly where birds sing,
That we may walk fittingly where grass is green,
O our Mother the Earth, O our Father the Sky.

Song of the Sky Loom (Tewa)

The Pueblo Indians of
the Southwest, in what
became New Mexico and
Arizona, were among
the first people to come into contact
with whites, encountering Spanish
explorers as early as the sixteenth
century. The name "pueblo" derives
from the Spanish word for "town" or
"village," reflecting the distinctive
attribute of peoples who lived in
fixed, permanent settlements. The
principal areas included the Hopi
lands, with several villages on three
mesas in northeastern Arizona;
Zuni, a pueblo about one hundred
miles further east, just across the
New Mexico border; and eighteen
pueblos, including Acoma, Isleta,

*Zuni Pueblo, with the mesa of Taaiya-
lone in the distance, New Mexico,
1870s. Albumen print by John
K. Hillers.*

In times of trouble, the inhabitants of
Zuni fled in defense to the high mesa of
Taaiyalone. Following the Pueblo
Revolt of 1680, they lived there for
twelve years, before moving to the site
of the present pueblo near the banks of
the river bearing its name. The view
across the terraced rooftops, with their
piles of drying corn, suggests a wealth
of activity and also illustrates many details of the massive adobe construction,
its chimneys, rafters, roof tiles, drain
spouts, and so forth. Just beyond the
town is an area of staked fencing, and
beyond that the walled-in gardens
where beans, red-peppers, and other
crops were grown. Zuni was the largest
of the pueblos: in 1880 its population
numbered 1,650.

and Taos, along the Rio Grande and its vicinity in northern central New Mexico.

Spanish rule was enforced harshly during colonization of the area in the seventeenth century, when missionaries built churches and secured converts. The Indians eventually rebelled and, during the so-called Pueblo Revolt of 1680, many missionaries, along with hundreds of colonists, were killed and the missions destroyed. Fearing reprisals by the Spanish, and under increased attack by nomadic raiders, including the Navahos, Apaches, and Utes, many Pueblo tribes moved their villages to more easily defended positions on the heights. The Hopi pueblos, situated atop a series of high mesas in northeast Arizona, were among these; they have remained there ever since. By contrast, the inhabitants of Zuni, after a limited time on a fortified mesa, eventually moved to the open river plain. Spanish, then Mexican, rule was reasserted in the region, but, by the time the U.S. acquired the Pueblo territory in the aftermath of the 1847 Mexican War, outside civil and religious authority

---

Dancers in the plaza of Zuni Pueblo, 1879. Frame from an albumen stereograph by John K. Hillers. ▷

Hopi clowns, probably 1880s. Albumen print by an unknown photographer. Among the pantheon of sacred spirits known as *kachinas* are a number that take the form of clowns, whose often ribald humor enlivens the sacred dances.

Three-story house, Oraibi Pueblo, Arizona, 1879. Albumen print by John K. Hillers.

Oraibi, meaning "place of the rock," is the largest and most important of the Hopi mesa villages in northeastern Arizona. Mortared stone masonry here replaced the adobe construction usual in valley pueblos. Three of the inhabitants are seen from the street that runs in front of their ancient house.

"A Back Wall," Walpi Pueblo, Arizona, 1870s. Albumen print by John K. Hillers. ▷

The man wears an old-style woven blanket; above him, near the top of the ladder, hangs a rabbit skin robe.

had become weak. The Zuni and Hopi Pueblos, in particular, had resisted "civilizing" pressures and retained their traditional culture and religion. Renewed attempts in the 1870s to missionize the Pueblos met with little success. A visitor in 1878 and in 1881 observed that the *kivas*, or ceremonial chambers, were well used, while many of the mission churches were in ruins.

Notwithstanding the aridity of the region, the economy was based on farming as well as on herding and hunting. Corn was the main crop grown; much of it was stored for drought years, along with beans, squash, chili peppers, and a variety of other fruits and vegetables. Domestic animals included sheep, goats, horses, and burros, while antelope, elk, rabbits, birds, and other small game were hunted.

The distinctive architecture of the pueblos was fashioned from local materials, either adobe, a mixture of earth and straw, or stone joined with mortar. The most expensive items were the ceiling timbers, which had to be cut and

transported many miles by mule. The houses were built with rooms stacked in several terraced stories; for defense reasons, the lower stories presented solid, impenetrable walls. Access was gained by ladders, which could be withdrawn in case of danger. One reached the upper stories also by ladder and, in the case of first-floor living rooms, by climbing down through an opening in the ceiling. As the likelihood of raids became more remote, doors and small windows began to appear on first floors. Terraces between the upper rooms served as work areas; ovens were built here, and corn and other produce left to dry. Many of the rooms were used to store food and might contain supply enough for several years — a precaution demanded by an undependable water supply. Thick walls helped insulate interiors against intense sun and retained heat during the cool nights. The rounded, bulbous chimneys were made of clay pots stacked on top of one another and covered with mud.

Although belonging to several different language groups, the Pueblo peoples developed remarkably similar life-styles and architecture. The outward serenity and the fascinating physical aspect of the

pueblos only hint at the intense, private life that existed within their confines. These villages housed tightly knit, independent, conservative communities, strongly resistant to change, in which ideals of communality outweighed the strong individualism found in many tribes elsewhere.

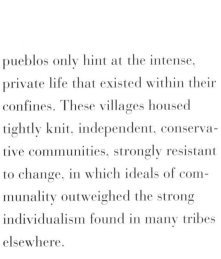

Hopi maidens, Walpi Pueblo, Arizona, 1870s. Frame from an original stereograph negative by John K. Hillers. The young women of marriageable age have whitened their faces with cornmeal and arranged their hair in "squash blossom" whorls to indicate their eligible status.

◁ *Carlota, a Tigua maiden, Isleta Pueblo, 1890. Gelatin silver print by Charles F. Lummis.*

The Pueblo political and social structure rested on a complex interweaving of clan, fraternity, and priesthood organizations. In addition to private houses, each of the clans and religious societies had its own *kivas*, where secret rites, jealously guarded from outsiders, were performed. The elaborate ceremonies, developed over generations, were directed to a large extent at sustaining crops and, to this day, form one of the most distinctive features of Pueblo culture. To a considerable extent, the region's aridity and lack of minerals saved it from western incursion, preserving the isolation of its peoples.

Taos Pueblo, New Mexico, 1880.
Frame from an albumen stereograph by
John K. Hillers.
Situated on a plateau at 7,000 feet before the Sangre de Cristo Mountains, Taos was the northernmost Pueblo town, and an important trade and administrative center in the nineteenth century. The houses of the northern quarter rise five stories behind an open courtyard containing "beehive" baking ovens.

HOPI SNAKE DANCE

Pueblo religious ceremonies were directed principally toward the growth of crops, especially crucial in the arid regions of the Southwest. One of the most important of these rites was the Snake Dance held every other year in August in most Hopi villages. Legend told that snakes and the Hopi people had common parents in the Snake Hero and Snake Maid, and that snakes had great power in influencing the gods to produce rain.

The public dance, in which priests carried live rattlesnakes in their mouths, was only the last part of a nine-day ritual, the preceding eight days being devoted to secret rites held in the *kivas*. Wearing headdresses and traditional kilted costumes, the dancers first circled the plaza and stamped on a wooden board set in the ground, to notify the spirits of the underworld that the dance was beginning. Lines of dancers chanted and swayed in unison, after which they separated into groups of three. Kneeling before a shelter of cottonwood boughs called a *kisi*, each dancer was given a snake to grasp in his mouth, after which he danced around the plaza four times, before dropping the snake and returning for another. The snake carriers were accompanied by assistants who, leaning across the

shoulder of the carrier, managed the snake with a short "whip" tipped with eagle feathers. After each snake had been carried, they were tossed upon a "six-directions picture" drawn in sacred cornmeal on the ground, then scooped up by the carriers, who raced down the slope of the mesa to release them at various points on the plain below.

At first, the Hopi tolerated the presence of photographers at the Snake Dance, but, as the government increased efforts to eradicate

Hopi Snake Dance at the village of Mishongnovi, Arizona, August 16, 1885. Albumen print by Victor Mindeleff. At left is the leafy shelter called kisi, where snakes collected for the ceremony are kept. Before it, a man grasps a tangle of snakes, while carriers with snakes in their mouths circle the plaza.

Native American religious rites, they prohibited whites from recording and even viewing it, lest the knowledge thus acquired be used against them.

GHOST DANCERS AND THE MASSACRE AT WOUNDED KNEE, 1890

The whole world is coming,
A nation is coming, a nation is coming,
The Eagle has brought the message to the tribe.
The father says so, the father says so.
Over the whole earth they are coming.
The buffalo are coming, the buffalo are coming.
The Crow has brought the message to the tribe,
The father says so, the father says so.

Sioux Ghost song

In the winter of 1888/89 rumors of a new religion originating in the West began to circulate among the Sioux living on their reservations in North and South Dakota. A delegation secretly visited the prophet of the new Ghost Dance doctrine, a Paiute named Wovoka living in Nevada. They were informed that a messiah had come who soon would cause the earth to be transformed and regenerated. When this happened, the white people would be destroyed and all Indians, living and dead, would be reunited in a world restored to its aboriginal state. The buffalo and game animals would return and Indian peoples live once more according to their ancient ways.

The Sioux were not alone. To Native Americans everywhere, the promise of deliverance from their present hardships and a renewal of their former lives, free of sickness and poverty, proved irresistible. So universal was the appeal of the Ghost Dance religion that it spread quickly through Indian territories in every western state.

To prepare people for the transformation of the world, and to help bring it about, believers were instructed to perform a communal dance which, because it linked them with the spirits of the dead, came to be known among the Sioux and other prairie tribes as the Ghost Dance. Participants in the dance

*Arapaho Ghost Dancers — "Inspiration,"
1890/91. Gelatin silver print by James
Mooney.*
More than the ceremony, Mooney's
photographs captured the essence of
that intense spirituality which had
always been a powerful element
of Native American life.

◁ *Arapaho Ghost Dancers, 1890/91.
Gelatin silver print by James Mooney.*

joined hands to form a ring; they
then moved in a circle with shuf-
fling side steps, singing songs that
told of the coming. As the ceremony
progressed, dancers could be seen
trembling and staggering. Some,
letting go of their companions'
hands, whirled about with their
arms flung outward, before falling
to the ground in a hypnotic trance.
In doing so, dancers were believed
to "die" and, on regaining con-
sciousness, were able to tell of their

experiences of meeting departed
loved ones in the afterworld. Many
brought back new songs from the
afterworld, and so the repertory of
Ghost songs constantly grew.

Although its form was new, the
Ghost Dance religion incorporated
elements from old rituals that had
been banned by the government.
In keeping with an admonition to
put aside all things connected with
whites, Indians brought out
costumes that had not been worn in

years. Many variations of the Ghost doctrine arose, as each tribe adapted it to its own traditions.

The Paiutes in Nevada, with whom the belief originated, held that the transformation of the world would take place when the Indians ascended the mountains and a great flood overwhelmed the white race. The Kiowa, Cheyenne, Arapaho, and other tribes in Oklahoma

Ghost Dance circle among Sitting Bull's band, Standing Rock Agency, North Dakota, 1890. Albumen print by Sam T. Clover for George W. Scott.
A hundred or more dancers appear to make up the dance circle, while others are seated to the side. Sitting Bull's tipi is seen to the right, and he was said to be the figure standing between it and the dancers. In the center rises the sacred tree, decorated with feathers, stuffed animals, and other sacred objects, that became part of the Sioux Ghost Dance. This feature led some whites to think that the ritual was a revival of the outlawed traditional Sun Dance.

When confronted by the authorities, Sitting Bull's band had moved their dance to a remote part of the reservation, away from outsiders. With a camera hidden at a distance, a Chicago reporter named Sam T. Clover took this unique view for the photographer at Fort Yates, who had it copyrighted. The secrecy of the ritual was jealously guarded from outsiders: when another photographer, Clarence More-ledge, tried surreptitiously to photograph the ceremony, an alarm was raised and his camera smashed out of his hand by angry participants wielding clubs.

◁ *Arapaho Ghost Dancers — "Rigid,"*
1890/91. Gelatin silver print by James
Mooney.
During the performance, some dancers
would fall into a trance and "die," at
which time they were able to communi-
cate with loved ones in the afterworld.

Arapahos praying during the Ghost
Dance ceremony, 1890/91. Gelatin
silver print by James Mooney.

believed that a new earth would
slide in from the west, covering the
present world and bringing with it
the old herds of elk and buffalo.
Sacred feathers worn by believers
would act as wings to carry them
over the sliding earth and onto the
new surface. After being uncon-

scious for four days, they would
awake among their old friends and
surroundings. According to one
Sioux version, the destruction of the
old world would come about
through earthquakes, floods, and
mudslides, accompanied by storms
and whirlwinds.

SITTING BULL

A famed warrior and medicine chief, Sitting Bull fled to Canada with his band of Hunkpapa Sioux after participating in the Battle of the Little Bighorn. Hunger eventually forced their return and surrender to white authorities in 1881. Confined to the reservation at Standing Rock, North Dakota, Sitting Bull remained irreconcilable to the imposition of the whites' civilization on his people, and his moral strength made him a rallying point for those who cherished traditional ways. He bitterly opposed the partitioning of the great Sioux reservation in 1889 and, in reference to the Indians who had signed the treaty allowing it, declared passionately: "Indians! There are no Indians left now but me." At Standing Rock he became an active supporter of the Ghost Dance religion. He was denounced by the authorities as a disturbing influence, and an order for his arrest was issued on December 15, 1890; Sitting Bull and some of his supporters were shot dead by native policemen when they resisted.

Sitting Bull (Tatonka Yotanka), 1885. Albumen print by David F. Barry. The lone white eagle feather symbolized the first coup Sitting Bull counted in battle, which occurred when he was fourteen years old.

In general, the people were taught to be worthy of this transformation by doing good works and acting peacefully, but among the Sioux, suffering and on the brink of starvation, the doctrine acquired some aggressive features. Adherents wore specially made Ghost shirts, which were ornamented with sacred feathers and symbols whose magical properties, they believed, made them impervious to enemies' bullets.

On the Sioux reservations the Ghost Dance became the rallying point for older, conservative Indians who felt bitter at the destruction of their former lives and the failure of the U.S. government to keep its promises. For years, the Indians' beef ration at the Dakota reservations had been steadily reduced until, in April 1890, the agent at Pine Ridge testified that it was less than half the amount stipulated by treaty. There were reports that the Sioux were becoming restless from hunger; this, in turn, led to rumors of a planned outbreak. That summer, some of the Sioux refused to accept meager rations and threatened the agent, who resigned when he saw that the government was doing nothing to remedy the situation.

Meanwhile, the rapidly spreading Ghost Dance had become increasingly worrisome to U.S. officials, who considered it a threat to the orderly process of "civilizing" the tribes. Attempts to ban it succeeded in some areas, but everywhere Indians resented what they saw as yet another attempt to deprive them of their freedom. In August 1890 about two thousand Sioux assembled at the principal dance ground at Pine Ridge. Native

The battlefield at Wounded Knee with frozen bodies of the victims, January 3, 1891. Albumen print by George Trager. Delayed by a blizzard and sporadic fighting, a civilian burial detail under military escort was sent five days after the massacre to collect the dead.

policemen were sent out to disperse them, but the dancers refused to move, some leveling guns and promising to defend their religion with their lives. The police withdrew and the dance continued. It spread to the other agencies. In early October, Chief Kicking Bear was invited by Sitting Bull to the Standing Rock reservation, and there inaugurated the dance among Sitting Bull's followers.

It was at this moment of spiraling tensions, in October 1890, that the veteran agent at Pine Ridge was replaced by an indecisive newcomer, D. F. Royer, nicknamed by the Indians Lakota Kokipa-Koshkala, or Young Man Afraid of Indians. On October 12 he reported that over half the six thousand Indians were performing the forbidden Ghost Dance and, believing the situation out of control, made the first of many pleas for military help. Outside the reservation the Ghost dancing had for a time been treated as something of a curiosity by local residents. Soon, however, the situation turned ominous as stories circulated that the Indians were planning an outbreak reminiscent of the Minnesota Uprising nearly thirty years earlier.

Tension continued to mount on both sides and, on October 31, Short Bull, who had personally seen the prophet Wovoka, told a large gathering of Indians at Pine Ridge that, in view of the whites' interference, the timing of the apocalypse would be moved up to within the next month, and that they should continue dancing. If the troops attacked, their magical Ghost shirts would protect them from the

The body of the Miniconjou leader Big Foot (Si Tanka) as it lay at Wounded Knee, January 3, 1891. Gelatin silver print by George Trager.

soldiers' bullets. "Whatever white men may tell you," he said, "do not listen to them."

With the situation seemingly beyond the control of the local agents, in November the military was summoned to prevent an uprising — a reaction to imagined dangers that were characterized by a local newspaper as "outlandish and improbable falsehoods." The first detachment of troops, accompanied by a squadron of newspaper reporters, arrived at Pine Ridge on November 19 and were soon reinforced by units of infantry, cavalry, and artillery. In all, nearly three thousand soldiers were stationed at the Pine Ridge and Rosebud agencies and in the surrounding areas. General Nelson A. Miles, a veteran of the Indian wars, was in command at Rapid City, South Dakota.

Alarmed by the arrival of troops, a large group from Rosebud and Pine Ridge, led by Short Bull, Kicking Bear, and others, sought refuge in the wild country, known as the Badlands, northwest of the reservations. Along the way they destroyed the homes of some Indians whom they believed to be friendly to the whites, and made off with much of the agency's cow herd. No whites were harmed. Eventually, the number of Indians fortified in the Badlands exceeded three thousand.

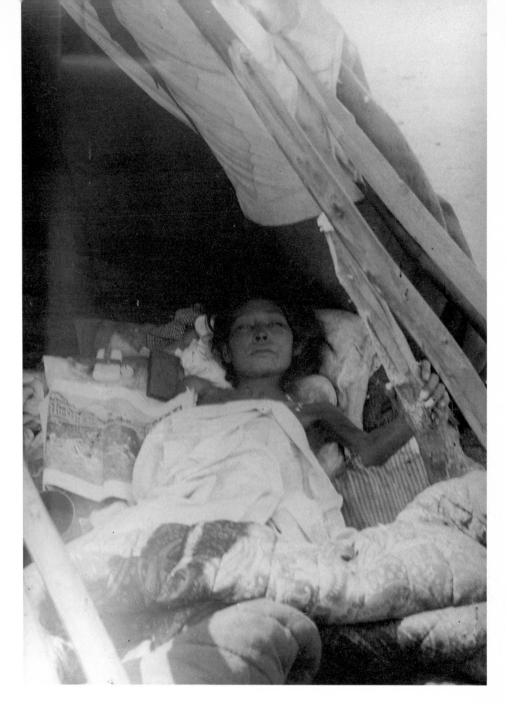

A victim of the Wounded Knee battle convalescing in the Miniconjou Camp, January 1891. Gelatin silver print by George Trager.
Immediately after the battle, when one of the Indian women wounded in the fight was told by her attendant that she would need to remove her Ghost Shirt, the woman replied: "Yes, take it off. They told me a bullet would not go through. Now I don't want it any more."

PLENTY HORSES

The story of the 22-year-old Brule Sioux named Plenty Horses demonstrated with brutal clarity the devastating effect that the process of "civilizing" — white man's education leading to the loss of native traditions — could have on some Indians. Plenty Horses had been educated at the Carlisle School in Pennsylvania (established in 1882), which zealously pursued a mission to transform Native American children into model white citizens. After graduating, the young man returned to his home on the Rosebud reservation and was present during the uprisings of 1890/91.

On January 7, 1891, while the Indians and military faced each other in a tense standoff after the Wounded Knee Massacre, the commander of a troop of Cheyenne army scouts, Lieutenant E.W. Casey, rode out with one of the scouts in an attempt to meet the Indian leaders. Chief Red Cloud sent a message to Casey warning him to keep away from the area, as he believed that some of the younger braves might do him harm. Not far from the main camp, Casey stopped to talk in a friendly way with several Indians, and was joined by Plenty Horses and a friend of his who happened by. As Casey turned to leave, Plenty Horses raised his

Plenty Horses (Tasunka Ota), 1891.
Gelatin silver print by L. T. Butterfield.

rifle and, without warning, shot Casey through the head from behind.

At his trial for murder, Plenty Horses explained his seemingly senseless deed: "I am an Indian. Five years I attended Carlisle and was educated in the ways of the white man. I was lonely. I shot the lieutenant so I might make a place for myself among my people. Now I am one of them. I shall be hung and the Indians will bury me as a warrior. They will be proud of me. I am satisfied."

Contrary to his prediction, Plenty Horses was acquitted of murder when the court ruled his deed an act of war.

By the beginning of December, with the agencies under military control, the Ghost Dance had been suppressed in areas near them; but much of the population remained out of reach, and the dance continued in the isolated areas of Sitting Bull's camp at Standing Rock and of Big Foot's camp on the Cheyenne River. During the following weeks, the situation took a precipitous slide toward disaster. Sitting Bull, considered one of the worst troublemakers, was ordered to be arrested. When Indian police, led by Lieutenant Bull Head, came for him at dawn on December 15, a vicious gunfight broke out between the police and about 150 of Sitting Bull's followers. Sitting Bull, along with his fourteen-year old son, Crow Foot, was killed, as were Lieutenant Bull Head, several other policemen, and members of Sitting Bull's band. The remaining Indians fled south to join the refugees in the Badlands. It was only a matter of days, however, before Hump, one of the principal leaders there, agreed to surrender to the military and helped persuade Sitting Bull's people to do likewise.

This left the Miniconjou chief, Big Foot, and his band of some four hundred followers as the only potential danger. Big Foot, too, was in the process of surrendering when rumors that the military meant to attack caused a panicky flight southward toward Pine Ridge. After five days, on December 28, the military once more caught up to the group, at Wounded Knee Creek. The events that followed are well known. The military and the Indians faced each other suspiciously, each fearing an attack from the other. The soldiers began to disarm the Indians, who gave up their guns grudgingly. Soldiers started to search the camp for more weapons, when a medicine man, who had begun to sing Ghost songs, stooped

"Indian Council in Hostile Camp": The great council among chiefs and leaders that settled the Indian war, 1891. Albumen print by John C. H. Grabill.

down and cast some dirt in the air. His gesture was part of the Ghost Dance ritual, but many of the soldiers took it as a signal to attack. With cruel synchrony, just then a gun went off in the Indian camp, fired by accident as a soldier tried to wrest a rifle from its owner. In an instant, fighting erupted and soon a desperate hand-to-hand battle engulfed the crowded camp. Shots fired at close range gave way to withering rifle fire from distant troops and then to exploding artillery shells. The Indians, most of them women and children, fled, many to a nearby ravine, but were cut down indiscriminately. When fighting ceased, hundreds of dead and dying littered the ground at Wounded Knee. No precise count was possible, but between 250 and 300 Indian dead seems a likely number. Scores more were wounded. Big Foot was killed in the fighting. His wife suffered wounds from which she later died. Twenty-five soldiers were killed and thirty-nine wounded, many evidently from friendly fire.

After news of the Wounded Knee Massacre reached them, many Sioux who had abandoned their stronghold in the Badlands retreated there once again, taking with them others who had always remained friendly to the whites. During the following days, a few attacks were launched against the military but, on January 15, 1891, the last Indians surrendered to General Miles. Six days later, the

General held a grand review of his combined troops, before dismissing them to other posts. Some of the Indian onlookers may have re- membered the simple message of one of the Sioux Ghost songs: "We shall live again, We shall live again."

Brule village near Pine Ridge, South Dakota, 1891. Albumen print by John C. H. Grabill.

Belying months of tension and their terrible conclusion, the Brule village at Pine Ridge outwardly assumed once more an air of timeless, tranquil beauty.

BIOGRAPHICAL NOTES
ON THE PHOTOGRAPHERS

References cited here in abbreviated form are given in full in the Selected Bibliography (pp.136-37).

DAVID F. BARRY

Born: Honeoye Falls, New York, March 6, 1855

Died: Superior, Wisconsin, March 6, 1934

Barry moved with his family to Osego in Columbia County, Wisconsin, in 1872. He settled in Bismarck, Dakota Territory, around 1874 and, from late 1878 or early 1879, became a protégé of Orlando S. Goff in the latter's photographic business. He ran Goff's Bismarck studio and, in October 1879, was noted as having "a fine collection of Indian photos" for sale. In 1880 he established himself independently at Fort Buford and, for the next several years, traveled to various military posts in Montana. He resettled in Bismarck in 1884, leasing Goff's old studio and opening a second gallery at Fort Yates. He made portraits of many Sioux leaders at Standing Rock Reservation — among them Chief Gall, with whom he became friends — and, in 1889, photographed some of the meetings between Indians and U.S. authorities that led to the breakup of the great Sioux reservation. He moved to Superior, Wisconsin, in 1890.

References: Thomas M. Heski, *Icastinyanka Cikala Hanzi: The Little Shadow Catcher — D. F. Barry, Celebrated Photographer of Famous Indians* (Seattle, 1978); Gray, 1978, pp. 11-15.

See pages 50, 114

CHRISTIAN BARTHELMESS

Born: Klingenberg, Germany, April 11, 1854

Died: Fort Keogh, Montana, April 10, 1906

Barthelmess settled in New York in the early 1870s, and joined the U.S Army in St. Louis in 1876. He spent his career as a professional soldier stationed at various forts in Arizona, New Mexico, Colorado, and, finally, Montana, where he occupied the position of chief musician of the 2nd Infantry Band on his retirement in 1903. His interest in photography began as a pastime, but eventually became a regular part of his military assignments. He photographed the personnel and military activities at his various posts, along with neighboring Indians, including members of the Navajo, Zuni, Hopi, Apache, and Cheyenne tribes. He encountered the latter after 1888, when he was posted to Fort Keogh, Montana, where many of his finest pictures were taken.

Reference: Maurice Frink with Casey E. Barthelmess, *Photographer on an Army Mule* (Norman, OK, 1965).

See page 49

EDWARD O. BEAMAN

Active c. 1865-75

After serving in the Civil War, Beaman practiced photography in New York, Ohio, and Illinois, before being hired for Major John Wesley Powell's second expedition down the Colorado River. He served with the expedition from May 1871, but quit at the beginning of 1872 after a disagreement with Powell. Several hundred of Beaman's negatives were retained by Powell, who ordered prints of 250 of them to be made by SAVAGE in Salt Lake City. The employee who actually did this work for Savage, James Fennemore, succeeded Beaman as expedition photographer, and was in turn succeeded by HILLERS. Beaman returned to Salt Lake City, where he equipped himself for a photographic tour of the Hopi mesas in Arizona, an excursion that furnished material for several illustrated articles published in 1872 and 1874. In 1873 Beaman was working in New York, whence he wrote Powell offering to produce stereographs from the expedition photographs and, later, to assist on a lecture tour that Powell was to undertake.

References: Johnson, 1990, p. 39; Don D. Fowler, *The Western Photographs of John K. Hillers — Myself in the Water* (Washington, D.C., 1989); F. Deniss Lessard, "E. O. Who?" *American Indian Art Magazine* 12 (1987), pp. 52-61; Hal G. Stephens and Eugene M. Shoemaker, *In the Footsteps of John Wesley Powell: An Album of... the Green and Colorado Rivers, 1871-72 and 1968* (Boulder, CO, 1987); William Culp Darrah, "Beaman, Fennemore, Hillers, Dellenbaugh, Johnson and Hattan," *Utah Historical Quarterly* 16/17 (Jan. 1948/Dec. 1949), pp. 491-503; *Appleton's Journal* 2 (1874), pp. 481-84, 513-16, 545-48, 590-93, 623-26, 641-44, 686, 689; *Anthony's Photographic Bulletin* 3 (1872), pp. 463-65, 703-5, 746-47.

See page 23

CHARLES MILTON BELL

Born: Virginia, 1848

Died: Washington, D.C., 1893

Member of a family of Washington photographers, Bell appears to have spent his entire professional life in that city, although he has also been tentatively identified with a C. B. Bell who was active from c. 1863 in New York and other eastern cities before moving to Washington in 1873. Working from various studio locations on Pennsylvania Avenue, Bell specialized in portraits of prominent Washingtonians, an activity that included photographs of Indian delegates to the capital.

References: Johnson, 1990, p. 49; Fleming, 1986, *passim*; J. Traill Taylor, "The Studios of America, No. 9: C. M. Bell's Gallery, Washington, D.C.," *Photographic Times* 13 (Sept. 1883), p. 474.

See page 15

DR. WILLIAM ABRAHAM BELL

Born: Clonmel, Ireland, April 26, 1841

Died: Surrey, England, June 6, 1921

The son of a distinguished London physician, Bell studied at Cambridge University, where he completed a medical degree in

1864. A few years later he gave up medicine and emigrated to America. Wishing to join a survey team of the Kansas Pacific Railroad, which was seeking a route westward from Salina, Kansas, Bell trained himself as a photographer in a matter of weeks with the help of the Philadelphian John Browne, so that he could fill the only position left available in the team. Once the trip was underway, he also became the survey physician. Bell photographed for the Kansas Pacific during 1867/68, traveling to the Pacific coast and back. He later wrote several accounts of his experiences in the West, but seems to have given up photography after the need had passed. Bell settled in Colorado Springs, Colorado, where he became active in the development of the Denver and Rio Grande Railroad and in a variety of mining and other companies throughout Colorado, Wyoming, Utah, and New Mexico. On his retirement in 1920 he returned to England.

References: Johnson, 1990, p. 50 (with incorrect dates); Current, 1978, p. 48ff.; Watson, 1948, p. 62; *National Cyclopaedia of American Biography*, vol. 25 (New York, 1935), p. 404; William A. Bell, *Wonderful Adventures: A Series of Narratives of Personal Experiences among the Native Tribes of America* (London and New York, 1874); *idem, New Tracks in North America* (London and New York, 1869).

See page 57

HENRY B. CALFEE

Born: Arkansas, January 3, 1848 (?)
Died: after 1900

Although described in an 1879 biographical note as being from Arkansas, the 1900 U.S. census records that Calfee was born in Kentucky in 1850. At the time of the census he had been married fifteen years to an Englishwoman and had two children. Calfee moved to Montana Territory in 1867 and was a painter, prospector, and miner for some years before he turned to photography. He made a specialty of views of Yellowstone Park, and was photographing there with his partner Catlin when the Nez Perce tribe under Chief Joseph passed through on its flight toward Canada in the summer of 1877. Calfee is recorded at Missoula in the 1870s, at Bozeman in 1879, and again at Missoula in 1886, when he was operating a studio and art store on Front Street. In 1884 he worked for a time in White Sulphur Springs: an advertisement

of October 9 announced the closure of his business, which had been housed in a "mammoth tent" on Hotel Square. He claimed to have "the most complete photograph outfit that has ever traveled in Montana, and [was] prepared to take photographs of persons, live stock, and out door scenery." In 1900 he was living at Bozeman.

References: Mrs. George F. Cowan, "Reminiscences of a Pioneer Life," *Contributions to the Historical Society of Montana* 4 (1903), pp. 179-80; *Weekly Missoulan*, Dec. 10, 1886; *Missoula County Times*, Dec. 8, 1886; *Rocky Mountain Husbandman*, Oct. 9, 1884, p. 6.

See page 29

DANA B. CHASE

Active c. 1873-97

Although he worked principally in Colorado, Chase is also recorded in New Mexico: at Raton, Springer, and Cimarron in May 1880, at Santa Fe from January 1884 to early 1885 and again from July 1888 to January 1892.

Reference: Richard Rudisill, *Photographers of the New Mexico Territory 1854-1912* (Santa Fe, NM, 1973), pp. 19-20.

See page 30

SAMUEL A. COHNER

Active: 1850s
Died: Cuba, 1869

Cohner practiced photography in Philadelphia and, later, at the James E. McClees studio in Washington, D.C., where a notable series of portraits of Indian delegates was produced in 1857/58. He moved to Havana, Cuba, in 1859. He was killed there ten years later in fighting between regular and volunteer Spanish troops. See also VANNERSON.

References: Glenn, 1981, p. 253; "Murder of Mr. Cohner," *Humphrey's Journal of Photography and the Allied Arts and Sciences* 20 (Feb. 15, 1869), p. 286; *Philadelphia Photographer* 6 (Feb. 1869), p. 64.

See page 41

THOMAS M. EASTERLY

Born: Guilford, Vermont, 1809
Died: 1882

Having begun his career as a calligrapher and teacher of penmanship, Easterly had moved to the Western frontier by 1845 to work as an itinerant photographer, initially in Iowa. He was associated with F. F. Webb in Liberty, Missouri, in 1846/47 and, in the latter year, established a daguerreotype studio of his own in St. Louis, where he practiced until the late 1870s, using the daguerreotype technique long after it had been abandoned by most others. Apart from many scenes in St. Louis, he is best known for the series of portraits of Indian leaders that he made during his first few years in Missouri.

References: Dolores A. Kilgo, "Preserving the Legends of the American Frontier: Daguerreotype Portraits by Thomas M. Easterly," *History of Photography* 13 (Apr.-June 1989), pp. 129-32; Carla Davidson, "The View from Fourth and Olive: A Remarkable Collection of Daguerreotypes by the St. Louis Photographer Thomas Easterly," *American Heritage* 31 (Dec. 1979), pp. 76-93; John C. Ewers, "Thomas M. Easterly's Pioneer Daguerreotypes of Plains Indians," *Missouri Historical Society Bulletin* 24 (July 1968), pp. 329-39.

See page 20

ADRIAN J. EBELL

Active: 1860s-70s
Died: April 1877

Ebell is first recorded in the early 1860s as engaged in performing magic lantern shows called "Phantasmagorical Exhibitions" that featured projected images of insects magnified many times. In 1862 he traveled with his assistant, Edward R. Lawton, from Chicago to the Santee reservation to obtain photographs of Indian life, and was there in mid-August when fighting forced his hasty retreat with a party of refugees. He subsequently fought against the Sioux as a member of Henry H. Sibley's army, resigning his commission in the fall of 1862. Ebell wrote a series of first-hand accounts of the war for the *St. Paul Daily Press* that were turned into a long article, containing engravings after his photographs, that appeared in the June 1863 issue of *Harper's Monthly Magazine*. He subsequently returned to school, graduating from the Sheffield Scientific School at Yale University in 1866 and obtaining a medical degree from Albany Medical College in 1869. Ebell's interest in photography, which focused on subjects of natural history, geology, and mining, seems to have continued in support of his writings and scientific studies. He published a natural history textbook, probably in the late 1860s, that went through several printings. By 1871 he had become director of The International Academy of Natural Science in St. Paul, Minnesota, which was later renamed The Ebell International Academy.

References: Johnson, 1990, p. 203; Alan R. Woolworth, "MHS Collections: Minnesota Indians—A Photographic Album," *Minnesota History* 47 (Fall 1981), pp. 292-95; "Historic Diary….," *Photographica* 11 (Dec. 1979), p. 13; Adrian J. Ebell, "The Indian Massacres and the War of 1862," *Harper's Monthly Magazine* 27 (June 1863), pp. 1-24.

See page 45

ALEXANDER GARDNER

Born: Paisley, Scotland, October 17, 1821

Died: Washington, D.C., December 1882

Gardner came to America permanently in 1856, intending to settle in the small utopian community of Clydesdale, Iowa, which he had helped found in 1849, together with his brother-in-law Robertson Sinclair. Learning on his arrival that disease had all but destroyed the community, he was forced to abandon his plans and took up residence in New York. Already an accomplished photographer, Gardner was immediately employed by Mathew Brady. Two years later he left New York to manage Brady's Washington, D.C., studio, in which he achieved notable success. Gardner worked for Brady during the first year of the Civil War but, after a dispute over credit for his photographs, he set up in competition with Brady. As a civilian attached to General George B. McClellan's headquarters staff, Gardner received the title Photographer to the Army of the Potomac and created a comprehensive record of the war's battlefields, fortifications, and leaders. In 1866 he published the impressive two-volume work *Gardner's Photographic Sketch Book of the War*, which included photographs taken by himself, O'SULLIVAN, and others. As proprietor of his own studio in Washington, Gardner became a celebrated portraitist, counting among his subjects many Indian

visitors to the city. In 1867/68 Gardner traveled through the West to photograph the construction of the transcontinental route of the Union Pacific Railroad. The following year he documented the treaty council held at Fort Laramie, Wyoming. A series of nearly one hundred stereographs deriving from this journey, with just over half representing Indian subjects, seems never to have been circulated commercially; the only known surviving set belonged once to the Peace Commissioner General C. C. Auger. Having become financially well-off through his photographic business and through real estate investments, Gardner increasingly turned his attention in later years towards philanthropic activity, particularly the Masonic Mutual Relief Association, an insurance program for workers.

References: Johnson, 1990, pp. 249-53; De-Mallie, 1981, pp. 42-57; Robert Sobieszek, *Alexander Gardner's Photographs Along the 35th Parallel* (Rochester, NY, 1976); Josephine Cobb, "Alexander Gardner," *Image* 7 (June 1958), pp. 124-36; Alexander Gardner, *Photographs of Red Cloud and Principal Chiefs of Dacotah Indians, Taken on Their Visit to Washington, D.C., May 1872, By Alexander Gardner for the Trustees of Blackmore Museum, Salisbury, England* (Washington, D.C., 1872); *idem, Gardner's Photographic Sketch Book of the War*, 2 vols. (Washington, D.C., 1865, 1866).

See pages 25, 35, 76-84

JOHN C. H. GRABILL

Active c. 1886-91

Grabill is documented in Sturgis, Dakota Territory, in October 1886 and, after 1887, at Hot Springs, Deadwood, and Lead. He also photographed in Wyoming and Colorado. His work includes scenes of military life, ranching and mining operations, and railroad construction, but his best known photographs are those he took at Pine Ridge Reservation in January 1891, recording events after the battle at Wounded Knee, and his portraits of Indian notables, including Plenty Horses. In the years immediately following Wounded Knee he published examples of both groups in a series titled "Indians and Indian Life," at which time he was operating the Grabill Portrait and View Company in Deadwood, SD, as well as being official photographer of the Black Hills & F.P.R.R. and Home Stake Mining Co.

References: Jensen *et al.*, 1991, p. 57ff.; "John C. Grabill's Photographs of the Last Conflict Between the Sioux and the United States Military, 1890-1891," *South Dakota History* 14 (1984), pp. 222-37; Current, 1978, pp. 212-13.

See pages 119-21

JOHN K. HILLERS

Born: Brinkum, Germany, December 20, 1843

Died: Washington, D.C., November 14, 1925

Hillers settled in New York in 1852. He joined the Union army in 1861 and, after re-enlisting several times, ended his military service as a sergeant in May 1870. He returned to New York for a few months before going to San Francisco to join his brother, a blacksmith. In the spring of 1871 he was in Salt Lake City, where he signed on as a boatman on Major John Wesley Powell's second expedition down the Colorado River. He learned photography from expedition photographers BEAMAN and James Fennemore, becoming proficient enough to be named head photographer by Powell in late summer 1872. Hillers spent the next two years photographing for Powell among the Hopi in Arizona and along the Colorado River. During a brief stay in San Francisco in 1873, he received some instruction from Carleton Watkins. Powell remained Hillers's patron and mentor throughout most of the photographer's later career, relying on his images to illustrate many articles and government reports produced for the U.S. Geological Survey and Bureau of Ethnology.

In the fall of 1874 Hillers accompanied Powell to Washington, D.C., and spent the next five years dividing his time between the capital and photographic field trips for Powell. In the spring and summer of 1875 he took photographs of the various tribes in Indian Territory; they were shown at the following year's Centennial Exhibition in Philadelphia and won him wide recognition. Early in 1876 he photographed the Hopi villages in Arizona.

In 1879 and several subsequent years Hillers made an extensive photographic survey for the studies of Pueblo Indians undertaken by Powell's newly founded Bureau of Ethnology, visiting and photographing at Zuni, Hopi, Laguna, Acoma, Cochiti, Santo Domingo, Santa Clara, San Ildefonso and elsewhere. In 1885 he became head of the photographic laboratory of the

U.S. Geological Survey and the Bureau of Ethnology. His activity after 1885 centered mainly on photographing members of Indian delegations to Washington, although he made further field trips to California's Yosemite Valley and Kings River region in 1892 and to several southern states in 1894.

References: Don D. Fowler, *The Western Photographs of John K. Hillers—Myself in the Water* (Washington, D.C., 1989); John K. Hillers, *"Photographed all the Best Scenery": Jack Hillers's Diary of the Powell Expedition, 1871-1875*, ed. Don D. Fowler (Salt Lake City, 1972).

See pages 32, 96/97, 99-101, 103, 104

LATON ALTON HUFFMAN

Born: Iowa, 1854

Died: Miles City, Montana, December 28, 1931

Huffman began learning photography in 1865 from his father, who operated a studio in Waukon, Iowa. He subsequently worked under Frank Jay Haynes. In 1878 he opened a studio at Fort Keogh, Montana Territory, where he photographed military personnel and many Indian notables. In 1880 he established a studio at Miles City, Montana, which he operated until 1890. Determined to record the fast vanishing frontier, which he loved, Huffman also traveled widely on expeditions into the surrounding country, photographing the towns, the landscape, and the remnants of the huge buffalo herds that had once roamed the area. He later worked in California and in Chicago, before returning to Montana in 1896. After operating a studio briefly in Billings, he once again established himself in Miles City, where he practiced until 1905. Thereafter, he continued to market his popular photographs until the end of his life.

References: Mark H. Brown and W. R. Felton, *Before Barbed Wire: L. A. Huffman,* *Photographer on Horseback* (New York, 1956); *idem, The Frontier Years: L. A. Huffman, Photographer of the Plains* (New York, 1955).

See pages 27, 70

WILLIAM HENRY JACKSON

Born: Keesville, New York, April 4, 1843

Died: New York City, June 30, 1942

Jackson began his photographic career in the 1850s in upstate New York and in Vermont prior to serving, from 1862 to 1865, with the 12th Vermont Infantry in the Civil War. In 1865 he went West, hoping to develop his skills as a draftsman and water-colorist while he earned his living doing odd jobs. The following year he established a photographic studio with his brother Edward in Omaha, Nebraska, and made short expeditions to photograph Native Americans living in the area. In 1869 he took photographs along the route of the Union Pacific Railroad and met Ferdinand Vandiveer Hayden, who offered him a job as photographer for his Geological Survey. Jackson's service with the Hayden Survey lasted from 1870 to 1879, during which time he worked in many of the western territories. His prolific talent made his name synonymous with the dazzling landscape of the American West. Among his best known photographs are the views he made in 1871 of the Yellowstone region, which was designated America's first National Park the following year. His government work included many photographs of Native American subjects and, in 1877, he catalogued the photographic collection of the Department of the Interior, which was later transferred to the Bureau of Ethnology. Jackson's photographs appeared in numerous publications relating to government surveys, as well as in private publications of the 1880s and 1890s, and remained popular throughout his life. In 1879 he opened a studio in Denver, Colorado, and from there continued to make frequent photographic expeditions to the West. In the 1880s and 1890s he worked for several railroad companies to document their new routes. Beginning in 1895, he traveled throughout the world for nearly two years, sending back regular illustrated articles to *Harper's Weekly*. In 1897 he became part owner of the Detroit Publishing Company, which he helped operate until its demise in 1924. Jackson enjoyed a long life and an extremely productive career, during which, according to one estimate, he created over fifty-four thousand glass negatives.

References: Johnson, 1990, pp. 335-44; Peter B. Hales, *William Henry Jackson and the Transformation of the American Landscape* (Philadelphia, 1988); Beaumont Newhall and Diana E. Edkins, *William H. Jackson* (Hastings-on-Hudson, NY, 1974); Aylesa Forsee, *William Henry Jackson: Pioneer Photographer of the West* (New York, 1964); Leroy R. Hafen and Ann W. Hafen (eds.), *The Diaries of W. H. Jackson, Frontier Photographer* (Glendale, CA, 1959); Clarence S. Jackson, *Picture Maker of the Old West: William Henry Jackson* (New York, 1947); William Henry Jackson, *Time Exposure: The Autobiography of William Henry Jackson* (New York, 1940); William H. Jackson with Howard R. Driggs, *William H. Jackson: The Pioneer Photographer* (Yonkers, NY, 1929).

See pages 16, 19, 53, 54, 58, 59, 88-92

CHARLES FLETCHER LUMMIS

Born: Lynn, Massachusetts, March 1, 1859

Died: Los Angeles, November 25, 1928

Lummis attended Harvard University from 1878 to 1881, subsequently embarking on a career as writer and editor. In 1884 he decided to walk the entire route from Cincinnati, where he was living at the time, to Los Angeles, making the trip in just under five months. He wrote during his travels for the *Los Angeles Times* and continued to work for them as a writer and as City Editor until 1887. That year he suffered a paralytic stroke and went to New Mexico to recuperate, eventually residing for four years in the pueblo of Isleta. Lummis took up photography in the mid-1880s and produced most of his finest work between 1888 and 1900, in connection with his studies of the Pueblo Indian and Hispanic cultures of the Southwest. He recalled that, while at Isleta, he had to accustom the residents to photography gradually, for "they believed that the photograph was taken not only of them, but *from* them; and that, with enough prints, they would waste away to nothingness." From 1888 to 1892 Lummis accompanied the anthropologist Adolph F. Bandelier on expeditions throughout the Southwest and, in 1892/93, to Peru. In 1888/89 Lummis wrote a series of articles entitled "My Brother's Keeper," in which he utilized his Pueblo portraits as a form of social documentary. He was, in fact, a highly prolific writer, responsible for many hundreds of books, articles, poems, and translations. In addition to pursuing historical research, Lummis became an energetic crusader for Indian rights, founding the Sequoya League, an Indian rights organization, in 1902. In 1907 he set up the Southwest Museum in Los Angeles, which now houses over five thousand of his glass negatives.

References: Daniela Moneta (ed.), *Charles F. Lummis: The Centennial Exhibition Commemorating His Tramp Across the*

William Henry Jackson with his equipment, Echo Canyon, Utah, 1869. Albumen print by an unknown photographer.

Charles F. Lummis with friends at Enchanted Mesa, near Acoma Pueblo, 1898. Silver gelatine print by Mrs. David Starr Jordan.

Continent (Los Angeles, 1985); Bradley B. Williams, "Charles F. Lummis: Crusader with a Camera," *History of Photography* 5 (July 1881), pp. 207-21; Mary A. Sarber, *Charles F. Lummis: A Bibliography* (Tucson, 1977); Turbese Lummis Fiske and Keith Lummis, *Charles F. Lummis: The Man and His West* (Norman, OK, 1975); Charles F. Lummis, *Mesa, Canon, and Pueblo* (New York, 1925); *idem, A Tramp Across the Continent* (New York, 1892).

See pages 26, 102

VICTOR MINDELEFF

Active 1880s-90s

A surveyor, photographer, and author, Mindeleff was employed by the U.S. Geological Survey, together with his brother Cosmos, to record the pueblos of Arizona and New Mexico and nearby archaeological sites.

References: Fleming, 1986, p. 140; Victor Mindeleff, *A Study of Pueblo Architecture: Tusayan and Cibola*, 8th Annual Report of the Bureau of Ethnology, 1886-1887 (Washington, D.C., 1891), pp. 13-228.

See page 105

JAMES MOONEY

Born: Richmond, Indiana, February 10, 1861
Died: December 22, 1921

Mooney was a professional ethnologist who used photographs as an aid to his researches. Fascinated by Indian life from an early age, he was able to secure a job in the Smithsonian Institution's Bureau of Ethnology in 1886. His first studies were of the Cherokees of North Carolina, and he was preparing to go to Indian Territory to continue this research when news of the Ghost Dance religion changed his purpose. Most surviving information about the Ghost religion, both written and visual, is owed to Mooney's field research. His study among the Cheyenne, Arapaho, Kiowa, Comanche, Apache, Caddo, Wichita, Paiute, Sioux, and other tribes began in December 1890 and lasted four years. During this time he traveled widely to interview, observe, and participate in the Ghost Dance ceremonies. In 1892 he even visited the prophet Wovoka. In addition to his writings, Mooney made use of a hand-held Kodak camera to record participants in the Dance. His later work included a study of the religious movement centering around the eating of peyote cactus, which resulted in the founding of the Native American Church. Mooney helped draft the charter of the Church in 1919 and, as a result of his advocacy of the peyotists, was recalled to Washington. At his death he left behind many unpublished field notes on peyote religion and other subjects.

References: L. G. Moses, *The Indian Man: A Biography of James Mooney* (Urbana, IL, 1984); Mooney, 1896.

See pages 108, 109, 112, 113

STANLEY J. MORROW

Born: Richland County, Ohio,
May 3, 1843
Died: Dallas, Texas, December 10,
1921

Morrow served in the Union army as member of Company F, Seventh Wisconsin Regiment, from September 1861 and fought in several of the war's major battles, including Fredericksburg, Antietam, and Gettysburg. In April 1864 he was transferred to the Volunteer Relief Corps at Point Lookout Prison, Maryland; during his five months there, he reportedly learned photography as an assistant to Mathew Brady. Morrow left the army in September 1864 and was married at Lodi, Wisconsin, on December 31 of the following year. In 1868 he and his wife moved to Yankton, Dakota Territory, where he operated a photography studio until 1883. In addition to recording local notables and events, he spent much time traveling throughout the Upper Missouri region, working at various towns and army posts. Among his photographs are scenes of steamboat traffic along the Missouri River. In 1883 Morrow moved to Geneva, Florida, and in 1888 he opened a studio in Atlanta, Georgia. Many of his negatives were lost in a fire around 1889.

References: Robert G. Duncan, "The Sioux War of 1876, Part 3: The Army Victorious," *Photographic Historian* 6 (Winter 1985/86), pp. 10-23; Paul L. Hedren, *With Crook in the Black Hills: The Photographic Legacy of Stanley Morrow* (Boulder, CO, 1985); Gray, 1978, pp. 8-10; Wesley R. Hurt and William E. Lass, *Frontier Photographer Stanley J. Morrow's Dakota Years* (Vermillion, SD, and Lincoln, NE, 1956).

See pages 36, 37, 68, 69, 71, 85, 93

TIMOTHY O'SULLIVAN

Born: c. 1840
Died: Staten Island, New York,
January 14, 1882

While still in his teens, O'Sullivan trained in New York under Mathew Brady and photographed for him during the early stages of the Civil War, before moving to Washington, D.C., to work for GARDNER in 1862. O'Sullivan's exceptional talent made him one of the most successful and prolific photographers of the war and, later, of the Western frontier. From 1867 to 1869, and again in 1871, he was photographer for the U.S. Geological Survey of the Fortieth

Parallel under Clarence King; in 1870 he was in Panama with the Selfridge expedition to find a canal route linking the Pacific and Atlantic oceans; and from 1871 to 1873 he accompanied the Wheeler Survey through parts of Nevada, Arizona, Utah, New Mexico, and Montana. O'Sullivan returned to Washington in 1875 to work for the Army Corps of Engineers. In 1880 he was named Photographer of the Treasury Department but, suffering from the effects of tuberculosis, was forced to resign in March 1881 and died shortly thereafter.

References: Johnson, 1990, pp. 467-70; William Brey, "O'Sullivan's Indians: The Wheeler Expeditions— 1871 through 1874," *Stereo World* 11 (July/Aug. 1984), pp. 14-21; Rick Dingus, *The Photographic Artifacts of Timothy O'Sullivan* (Albuquerque, 1982); Joel Snyder, *American Frontiers: The Photographs of Timothy O'Sullivan, 1867-1874* (New York, 1981); James D. Horan, *Timothy O'Sullivan: America's Forgotten Photographer* (New York, 1966); Beaumont Newhall and Nancy Newhall, *T. H. O'Sullivan, Photographer* (Rochester, NY, and Fort Worth, TX, 1966).

See page 31

CHARLES R. SAVAGE

Born: Southampton, England,
August 16, 1832
Died: Salt Lake City, Utah, 1909

Savage came to America in 1858 and worked briefly in New York City for Elder Stenhouse, before moving the next year to Nebraska. He opened a studio in Council Bluffs, Iowa, in 1860 and then moved to Salt Lake City, Utah, where he became partner in the Pioneer Art Gallery. In 1862 he joined George Martin Ottinger in the firm of Savage & Ottinger, which existed until about 1870. Charles W. Carter, James Fennemore, and George E. Anderson were among the photographers who worked for Savage in the 1860s and 1870s. As a practicing Mormon, Savage photographed Mormon leaders and activities in the Salt Lake City area, and in 1870 he accompanied Brigham Young on a trip through Zion Canyon. His work often appeared in photographic and news journals. A fire destroyed his studio in 1883, but he continued in business, and in 1888 was reportedly publishing *The Busy Bee*, a magazine devoted to home industry that included photographic topics. He retired in 1906, leaving the studio operations to his sons.

References: Johnson, 1990, pp. 553-54; C. R. Savage, "How to be a Successful Photographer," *Photographic Times* 21 (Dec. 25, 1891), p. 668.

See page 17

GEORGE W. SCOTT

Active c. 1890

Based at Fort Yates, North Dakota, Scott took the only known photograph of Sitting Bull's band performing the Ghost Dance, which he copyrighted on February 20, 1891.

See pages 110/11

WILLIAM STINSON SOULE

Born: Turner, Maine, August 28,
1836
Died: 1908

Raised in New England, Soule joined his elder brother, John P., in the Soule Photographic Company in the Boston suburb of Melrose, Massachusetts, before enlisting in the Union army in 1861. Severely wounded in 1862 at the Battle of Antietam, he spent the remainder of the war as a clerk in Washington, D.C. After the war he operated a studio in Chambersburg, Pennsylvania, until it was destroyed by fire. Motivated in part by a wish to improve his health, he moved to the West early in 1867, taking with him photographic outfits for both landscape and portrait work. At Fort Dodge, Kansas, he was hired as chief clerk of the post store, but also sporadically practiced photography. In January 1868 *Harper's Weekly Magazine* published a wood engraving after his photograph of a local hunter lying dead and scalped near the fort. Soule left for Camp Supply shortly after its foundation in November 1868 and was there in March 1869 to photograph the Cheyenne chiefs who had been brought there as prisoners of Custer's Seventh Cavalry. In late 1869 or early 1870 Soule moved to Fort Sill in Oklahoma Territory and, possibly under contract to the U.S. Army, produced a series of photographs of the fort during its early construction phases. For the next four or five years he maintained a gallery at Fort Sill and photographed many famous Indian leaders who came to the fort. In addition to studio portraits, Soule also ventured into the field to photograph villages of various tribes— Comanche, Arapaho, Kiowa, Kiowa-Apache, Wichita, and Caddo— who were established in the vicinity. A number of Soule's Fort Sill photographs were copyrighted in 1873 and sold by his elder brother, John, in Boston. In the later years of the century Soule's photographs were used to illustrate a number of books about the southern Plains tribes. Soule returned to Boston permanently in late 1874 or early 1875. He married, and continued the family photographic business under the Soule name, but in partnership with W. D. Everett. In the early 1890s he was still advertising "photographs of Indian celebrities" from his studio at 363 Washington Street. He retired in 1902.

References: Thomas W. Kavanagh, "Whose Village?: Photography by William S. Soule, Winter 1872-1873," *Visual Anthropology* 4 (Mar. 1991), pp. 1-24; Johnson, 1990, p. 585; Russell E. Belous and Robert A. Weinstein, *Will Soule: Indian Photographer at Fort Sill, Oklahoma 1869-74* (Los Angeles, 1969); Nye, 1968, pp. viii-xiv.

See pages 51, 52, 63, 72/73

GEORGE E. TRAGER

Born: Gefell, Germany, 1861
Active: Chadron, Nebraska,
c. 1889-95

Documented in Wisconsin in 1882, Trager studied photography in Whitewater. By 1888 he had opened a studio in Mazomanie in partnership with Frederick Kuhn. They moved to Chadron, Nebraska, in the fall of 1889 and worked together until January 1, 1891, when Trager bought out Kuhn. Trager traveled the nearby region photographing the scenery, but by the fall of 1890 had begun to take an active interest in the events attracting attention at the Pine Ridge and Rosebud reservations. He made numerous trips to Pine Ridge, where he photographed the troops who had arrived in response to the presumed Ghost Dance threat, and he served as something of an intermediary, relaying news, or the lack of it, from the reservation to the citizens of Chadron. Trager photographed the casualties being treated in the aftermath of the Wounded Knee Massacre and, on January 3, accompanied the burial detail to the battle site, where he photographed the dead victims and their interment. Later that month he took views of Sioux councils and of their camps and military activities. On January 9, 1891, a local newspaper, *Chadron Advocate*, reported that the eleven views taken by Trager of the battlefield were "attracting intense attention at his studio." Trager

proceeded to market these photographs aggressively, and with great, if short-lived, success, through the Northwestern Photographic Company at Chadron. For a while, the company had a half-dozen assistants to help in printing and employed traveling salesmen to take orders throughout the country. Trager sold his studio in 1892 and later worked briefly in Yellowstone National Park, before forming another partnership, with F. M. Steadman, in Fremont, Nebraska. His activities after 1893 are undocumented.

References: Jensen *et al.*, 1991, p. 39ff.; Lynn Marie Mitchell, "George E. Trager: Frontier Photographer at Wounded Knee," *History of Photography* 13 (Oct.-Dec. 1989), pp. 303-9.

See pages 115-17, 130/31.

BENJAMIN FRANKLIN UPTON

Born: 1818
Died: after 1901

Upton operated a daguerreotype studio in Maine from 1844. In 1856 he moved to St. Anthony, Minnesota, living at Big Lake. He photographed many local views and traveled frequently in search of new subjects. At some point he seems to have worked in partnership with James E. Martin of St. Paul, Minnesota. Upton's work in the 1860s included field photographs of Ojibwa Indians and, in 1862, he photographed Sioux prisoners held at Fort Snelling after the Minnesota Uprising. Other series included "Winter in the Pine Forests of Minnesota" and "Views of the Upper Mississippi." He lived in St. Anthony from 1865 to 1875 and afterward settled in Florida, where he continued to work.

References: Bonnie G. Wilson, "Working the Light: Nineteenth Century Professional Photographers in Minnesota," *Minnesota History* 52 (Summer 1990), p. 51ff.; Alan R. Woolworth, "MHS Collections: Minnesota Indians—A Photographic Album," *Minnesota History* 47 (Fall 1981), pp. 292-95.

See page 44

JULIAN VANNERSON

Born: Virginia, c. 1826

One of several brothers who were professional photographers, Vannerson first worked in the Washington studio of Jesse H. Whitehurst in the early 1850s, before taking over his brother's gallery in that city in 1856. He was head of the James E. McClees studio in

1857/58, when a number of Indian delegations visiting the capital were photographed there. By the beginning of the Civil War he had moved to Richmond, Virginia, where he made portraits of famous leaders throughout the war. Not documented in Richmond for several years after 1866, he is recorded there again in 1875 as operator of the studios of David H. Anderson in Richmond and Norfolk. See also COHNER.

References: Johnson, 1990, p. 652; Glenn, 1981, p. 253.

See page 41

ORLOFF R. WESTMANN

Active c. 1871

In 1871 Westmann worked for the Englishman William Blackmore photographing Taos and Apache Indians at Taos, New Mexico. He operated a studio at Elizabethtown, New Mexico.

Reference: Fleming, 1986, pp. 211, 245.

See page 18

JOEL EMMONS WHITNEY

Born: Phillips, Maine, 1822
Died: St. Paul, Minnesota,
January 20, 1886

Whitney moved to St. Paul, Minnesota, in 1850 and was operating a daguerran studio there the following year. In 1852 he studied with Alexander Hesler in Galena, Illinois, and worked with him in Minnesota. By 1855 Whitney was advertising the benefits of the new wet-plate process. He is documented at various business locations in St. Paul throughout the 1850s. Whitney began photographing Native Americans before the Minnesota Uprising of 1862, but his best known images are those taken of participants in the uprising during their imprisonment at Fort Snelling. His subjects included Medicine Bottle, Cut Nose, Little Crow, and Little Six, and he also produced several images of women and children. Whitney was aided at various times by his wife and by the photographers Andrew Falkenshield and M. C. Tuttle. From 1867 he was assisted by ZIMMERMAN, who took over Whitney's business after ill health forced him to retire in 1871. Zimmerman continued to market Whitney's negatives under his own name. Whitney subsequently lived in Georgia and Tennessee, before returning to St. Paul in 1880.

References: Bonnie G. Wilson, "Working the Light: Nineteenth Century Professional Photographers in Minnesota," *Minnesota History* 52 (Summer 1990), p. 45ff.; Johnson, 1990, p. 693; Alan R. Woolworth, "MHS Collections: Minnesota Indians — A Photographic Album," *Minnesota History* 47 (Fall 1981), pp. 292-95; Newhall, 1954; "Indian Photographs," *Philadelphia Photographer* 3 (Feb. 1866), p. 64.

See pages 42, 48

GEORGE BENJAMIN (BEN) WITTICK

Born: Huntingdon, Pennsylvania, January 1, 1845

Died: Fort Wingate, Arizona, 1903

Taken to Moline, Illinois, by his parents in 1854, Wittick served with the First Minnesota Volunteers at Fort Snelling, Minnesota, during the Civil War. He then returned to Moline and, after learning from a man named Mangold, set up his own photographic business there. In 1878 he went to Santa Fe, New Mexico, working there (for the Atlantic and Pacific Railroad) and in northern Arizona. From 1880 he had galleries in Santa Fe and Albuquerque in partnership first with R. P. Bliss and then with R. W. Russell, but undertook photographic expeditions to the surrounding areas and to Mexico. In 1880 he was allowed to photograph the Snake Dance ceremony of the Hopi and, soon after, joined the party of archaeologist Colonel James Stevenson on a trip to the Grand Canyon, entering Supai Canyon to photograph the Havasupai Indians. From 1884 to 1900 Wittick operated a studio in Gallup, New Mexico. During these years he was variously reported to be photographing at Canyon de Chelly, Flagstaff, Fort Apache, and Wide Ruin in Arizona. He was in southern Arizona in 1885 and accompanied troops from Fort Wingate in their pursuit of Geronimo. He formed a partnership with J. C. Burge for a short time in 1885. In 1900 Wittick set up a studio at Fort Wingate, assisted by his son Archie.

References: Bruce Hooper, "Camera on the Mogollon Rim: Nineteenth Century Photography in Flagstaff, Arizona Territory, 1867-1916," *History of Photography* 12 (Apr.-June 1988), pp. 93-101; Richard Rudisill, *Photographers of the New Mexico Territory 1854-1912* (Albuquerque, 1973); Gar Packard and Maggy Packard, *Southwest 1880 with Ben Wittick, Pioneer*

Photographer of Indian and Frontier Life (Santa Fe, 1970); Richard Van Valkenburgh, "Ben Wittick: Pioneer Photographer of the Southwest," *Arizona Highways* 18 (Aug. 1942), pp. 36-39.

See page 28

CHARLES A. ZIMMERMAN

Born: Alsace, France, 1844

Died: St. Paul, Minnesota, 1909

Zimmerman moved to St. Paul, Minnesota, in 1856 and, while still in his teens, became assistant to WHITNEY. From 1862 to 1865 he served with the 6th Minnesota Volunteer Infantry Regiment in the Civil War and afterward returned to Whitney's studio, becoming a partner in 1870. Zimmerman purchased the business outright the next year, leading him to refuse an invitation to become photographer for John Wesley Powell's Colorado River expedition. His work won gold medals at the Centennial Exposition of 1876 in Philadelphia. In 1872 he opened a new studio in St. Paul where, in addition to portraits and landscape work, he sold photographic equipment and watercolors of his own making. He produced many photographs of the Minnesota landscape, sometimes working in an open boat. In remarks made before the National Photographic Association in 1873 Zimmerman confessed that he was forced to photograph bizarre and unusual subjects to cater for the "love of the sensational [that] is inherent in the masses," distinguishing this from what he considered true landscape art. That year he became partner, with his brother Edward O., in a photographic supply business that, from 1898 to 1900, published the photographic journal *Northwestern Amateur*.

References: Bonnie G. Wilson, "Working the Light: Nineteenth Century Professional Photographers in Minnesota," *Minnesota History* 52 (Summer 1990), p. 49ff.; Johnson, 1990, p. 719; C. A. Zimmerman, "Some Photographic Crises," *American Annual of Photography 1910* 24 (1910), pp. 110-13; idem, "Lighting and Posing," *Wilson's Photographic Magazine* 34 (Sept. 1897), pp. 401-9; idem, "Fifth Annual Meeting . . . On Landscape Photography," *Philadelphia Photographer* 10 (Sept. 1873), pp. 447-48.

See page 22

Little information was available to the author on L. T. BUTTERFIELD (active c. 1891, Sioux Falls, South Dakota: see page 118), CHARLES W. CARTER (active c. 1865-80, Salt Lake City, Utah, for a time in the firm of SAVAGE & Ottinger; see page 64), and DANIEL CADZO (active 1882, Fort Macleod, Alberta, Canada: see page 65).

Unknown photographer (foreground), possibly Clarence Moreledge, at the Wounded Knee battlefield, January 3, 1891. Albumen print by George Trager.

CHRONOLOGY

1800
Indian population estimated at 600,000 (Bureau of Indian Affairs). At the time of first European contact with North American Indians, most estimates set the figure at many millions.

1803
Louisiana Purchase from France adds to the United States 828,000 square miles of land from the Gulf of Mexico to the Canadian border and from the Mississippi River to the Rocky Mountains, placing many new tribes under U.S. dominion.

1803-1806
Expedition headed by Meriwether Lewis and William Clark journeys to the Pacific Ocean.

1813
Shawnee leader Tecumseh, after years of efforts to unite Indian tribes against European encroachment, is killed in the Battle of the Thames.

1816-1818
First Seminole War.

1819
Florida acquired from Spain.

1824
Bureau of Indian Affairs is organized within the War Department, to be taken over in 1849 by the Department of the Interior.

1830
Indian Removal Act calls for displacement of eastern Indians to a region west of the Mississippi designated as Indian Territory (present-day Oklahoma).

1832
Position of Commissioner of Indian Affairs created.
Black Hawk's War between the U.S. and Sauk and Fox tribes in Wisconsin and Illinois.

1837
In one of the worst outbreaks of European disease, a smallpox epidemic in the Upper Missouri River region decimates Mandan, Arikara, and Hidatsa tribes.

1838/1839
Cherokees forced to march the "Trail of Tears" as they are removed to Indian Territory; Choctaw, Chicasaw, Creek, Seminole (with the Cherokee, known as the Five Civilized Tribes), and other tribes are also relocated.

1845
Texas annexed. Florida granted statehood.

1848
Mexico cedes to the U.S. the territories of California, Nevada, and parts of New Mexico, Utah, Arizona, and Colorado. Wisconsin granted statehood.

1849
California Gold Rush.

1850s
The reservation system becomes widespread.

1853
Gadsden Purchase.

1860
Paiute War in Nevada.
1.4 million whites are living in the West; by 1890 the number will have increased to 8.5 million.

1861-1865
American Civil War. By this time most lands west of the Mississippi have been organized into territories. States added to the U.S. in the preceding decade include California, Oregon, Kansas, and Minnesota. Nevada is granted statehood in 1864.

1862
Santee Sioux Uprising in Minnesota results in the death of many hundreds of settlers and, eventually, in the banishment of most Sioux and Winnebago Indians from the state.

1863/1864
Navajo War led by Manuelito. Following their surrender in the spring of 1864, the Navajos undertake a forced evacuation, known as the "Long Walk," to a new home in Bosque Redondo, New Mexico.

1864
Massacre of Cheyennes and Arapahos at Sand Creek by Colorado volunteers under Colonel John Chivington.

1866
The Five Civilized Tribes are forced to cede the western half of Indian Territory to other tribes as a reprisal for some members' support of the Confederacy.
During a council at Fort Laramie, Red Cloud denounces U.S. plans to fortify the Bozeman Trail, which leads along the Powder River to the Montana mining country. Red Cloud becomes the leader of Sioux and allied tribes in fighting against white incursion.
In December an eighty-man battalion commanded by William J. Fetterman is annihilated by the Sioux near Fort Phil Kearny, in an action known as the Fetterman Massacre.

1867
Medicine Lodge Treaty assigns reservation lands in Indian Territory to Kiowas, Kiowa-Apaches, Comanches, Arapahos, and Cheyennes.
Nebraska granted statehood.
First of the four great U.S. government geographical and geological surveys begins: King Survey, 1867-79; Hayden Survey, 1870-79; Wheeler Survey, 1871-79; and Powell Survey, 1871-79.

1868
At Fort Laramie Treaty council the U.S. government agrees to abandon forts along the Bozeman Trail.
Fourteenth Amendment excludes Indians from the electoral process.
Officials allow the Navajos to return to their homeland on a reservation created in New Mexico, Arizona, and Utah.

1868/1869

Southern Plains War involving Cheyennes, Arapahos, Comanches, Kiowas, and Sioux.

1869

The Central Pacific and Union Pacific railroads join at Promontory Point, Utah, forming the first continuous transcontinental railroad line.

Beginning of President Grant's "Peace Policy" toward Indians.

Ely Parker (Donehogawa), a Seneca, is appointed Indian Commissioner: political enemies force him to resign in 1871.

1871

Congress enacts law depriving Indian tribes of separate nation status. Existing treaties are recognized, but henceforth Indians are treated as individuals subject to U.S. law.

1872/1873

Modoc War in California.

1874

Angered at the slaughter of their buffalo herds, Cheyennes, Arapahos, Kiowas, and Comanches under Quanah Parker attack professional buffalo hunters at Adobe Walls, but are repelled.

1874/1875

Red River War in the southern Plains, involving Comanches, Kiowas, and Cheyennes. Kiowa leader, Lone Wolf, and Comanche leader, Chief Quanah Parker, are forced to surrender early in 1875 at Fort Sill, Oklahoma.

1876

Black Hills War erupts after miners invade Sioux treaty lands. United forces of Sioux, Cheyennes, and Arapahos, led by Crazy Horse, Sitting Bull, and Gall, annihilate General George A. Custer's command at the Battle of the Little Bighorn River. In the following fall and winter the scattered Indian forces suffer a series of decisive defeats. Dull Knife and Crazy Horse surrender, and Sitting Bull takes refuge in Canada, in 1877.

1877

Nez Perces War and flight of the Nez Perces under Chief Joseph.

1878/1879

Flight of Northern Cheyennes from Indian Territory, led by Little Wolf and Dull Knife; most of the tribe dies in the resulting fighting.

1879

Founding of Smithsonian Institution's Bureau of Ethnology.

Carlisle Indian School, an institution designed to prepare Indian students for full assimilation, is founded in Pennsylvania.

1881

Sitting Bull leaves Canada and surrenders with his band at Fort Buford, Dakota Territory.

Geronimo flees San Carlos Reservation.

1886

Surrender of Geronimo effectively ends Apache Wars.

1887

General Allotment Act (Dawes Act) reapportions tribal reservation lands to Indians as individuals, opening millions of "surplus" acres for white settlement.

1889

Partitioning of the Great Sioux Reservation in Dakota.

1889/1890

South Dakota, North Dakota, Montana, Washington, Idaho, and Wyoming are granted statehood.

1890

Ghost Dance religion spreads throughout the U.S. Indian population. The U.S. Army occupies the Dakota Sioux reservations to prevent a feared insurrection.

Sitting Bull is killed during arrest attempt by native policemen.

On December 29 the U.S. Seventh Cavalry fights Sioux Ghost Dance adherents under Big Foot at Wounded Knee, Pine Ridge Reservation, South Dakota, resulting in over three hundred Indian deaths. On January 15, 1891, the last resisters surrender to General Nelson A. Miles.

The U.S. Census records the Indian population as 248,253.

NOTES

INTRODUCTION:
PHOTOGRAPHING THE WESTERN
FRONTIER, c. 1865-1890

p. 13 *"The Great Spirit has made this country for us"*: quoted in *Report of a Reconnaissance made by Lieut. Henry E. Maynadier, 10th Infantry, in the Country about the Yellowstone River in the Summer of 1860*, p. 77 (manuscript journal in the William Franklin Raynolds Papers, The Beinecke Rare Book and Manuscript Library, Yale University).

p. 14 *"We knew that more and more"*: preface to the 1872 edition of Francis Parkman, *The Oregon Trail: Sketches of Prairie and Rocky Mountain Life* (1847; Random House edition, New York, 1949), pp. xvii-xviii.

p. 14 *"rescue from oblivion"*: George Catlin, quoted in Ron Tyler, *American Canvas: The Art, Eye, and Spirit of Pioneer Artists* (New York, 1983), p. 34.

p. 16 (caption) *"the paradise of the Indian"*: *Report of a Reconnaissance made by Lieut. Henry E. Maynadier, 10th Infantry, in the Country about the Yellowstone River in the Summer of 1860*, p. 104 (manuscript journal in the William Franklin Raynolds Papers, The Beinecke Rare Book and Manuscript Library, Yale University).

p. 18 *"even the 'Sons Of The Forest'"*: quoted in Bonnie G. Wilson, "Working the Light: Nineteenth Century Professional Photographers in Minnesota," *Minnesota History* 52 (Summer 1990), p. 42ff.

p. 18 *"a beautiful Indian girl"*: Solomon Nunes Carvalho, *Incidents of Travel and Adventure in the Far West...* (New York, 1857; Centenary Edition, Philadelphia, 1954), pp. 128-29.

p. 19 (caption) *"were on their way to the Wind River Valley"*: Jackson, *Descriptive Catalogue*, p. 76.

p. 21 *"soon, my one-horse studio"*: William Henry Jackson, *Time Exposure: The Autobiography of William Henry Jackson* (New York, 1940), p. 173.

p. 22 *Dr. Ferdinand Vandiveer Hayden noted*: in William Henry Jackson, *Descriptive Catalogue of Photographs of North American Indians*, U.S. Department of Interior Miscellaneous Publication No. 9 (Washington, D.C., 1877), p. iii.

p. 22 *Evidence of this is provided by Jackson's description*: Leroy R. Hafen and Ann W. Hafen (eds.), *The Diaries of William Henry Jackson, Frontier Photographer* (Glendale, CA, 1959), pp. 290-91.

p. 26 *The equipment carried by Jackson*: Robert Taft, *Photography and the American Scene: A Social History, 1839-1889* (New York, 1938; repr. 1964), p. 309.

p. 26 *Similar equipment carried by Beaman*: Frederick S. Dellenbaugh, *A Canyon Voyage: The Narrative of the Second Powell Expedition down the Green-Colorado River from Wyoming, and the Exploration of Land, in the Years 1871 and 1872* (New York, 1908; repr. Tucson, 1984), p. 58.

p. 26 (caption) *"The grave was new"*: quoted in Mark H. Brown and W. R. Felton, *The Frontier Years: L. A. Huffman, Photographer of the Plains* (New York, 1955), p. 257.

p. 29 *"for the purpose of obtaining"*: manuscript diary of Edwin R. Lawton, p. 14; Minnesota Historical Society.

p. 30 *"I had much difficulty in making pictures"*: letter of June 30, 1866, from Fort Laramie; quoted in "Photography Among the Indians," *Philadelphia Photographer* 3 (Aug. 1866), pp. 239-40.

p. 32 *"[The Indians] looked very wild"*: letter of July 29, 1866, from Fort Phil Kearney; quoted in "Photography Among the Indians, II," *Philadelphia Photographer* 3 (Nov. 1866), p. 339.

p. 32 *"[I] arrived here"*: ibid., p. 339.

p. 32 *Met in the field*: for an obituary of Glover, see *Philadelphia Photographer* 3 (Dec. 1866), p. 371, and for letters from the West describing his death, "The Fate of a Frank Leslie 'Special'," *Frank Leslie's Illustrated Newspaper* 23 (Oct. 27, 1866), p. 94.

p. 34 *"The dance was our religion"*: quoted in James Mooney, *The Ghost Dance Religion and the Sioux Outbreak of 1890*, Part 2, 14th Annual Report of the Bureau of Ethnology, 1892-1893 (Washington, D.C., 1896), p. 1060.

p. 34 *"About the last of the busy sojourners"*: quoted in Elmo Scott Watson, "Photographing the Frontier," *The Westerner's Brandbook* (Chicago) 4 (Jan. 1948), p. 66.

p. 37 *"views taken by me"*: *Yankton Press*, Sept. 27, 1881; quoted in Wesley R. Hurt and William E. Lass, *Frontier Photographer Stanley J. Morrow's Dakota Years* (Vermillion, SD, 1956), p. 1.

MINNESOTA UPRISING, 1862

p. 39 *"The Indians wanted to live"*: quoted in Kenneth Carley, "As Red Men Viewed It: Three Indian Accounts of the Uprisings," *Minnesota History* 38 (Sept. 1962), p. 129.

p. 40 *"Many of the whites"*: quoted ibid., p. 130.

p. 40 *"You may kill one"*: quoted in Kenneth Carley, *The Sioux Uprising of 1862* (Saint Paul, MN, 1976), p. 11.

p. 40 *"Taoyateduta"*: quoted in "Ta-oya-te-duta Is Not a Coward," *Minnesota History* 38 (1962), p. 115.

p. 42 *"Myrick is eating grass"*: quoted in Carley, "As Red Men Viewed It," p. 135.

WARRIORS

p. 47 *"I shall vanish and be no more"*: quoted in Alice Fletcher and Francis LaFlesche, *The Omaha Tribe*, 27th Annual Report of the Bureau of American Ethnology, 1905-1906 (Washington, D.C., 1911), p. 475.

p. 48 *"When I think of all the people"*: quoted in Alice C. Fletcher, *The Hako: A Pawnee Ceremony*, 22nd Annual Report of the Bureau of American Ethnology, 1900-1901, part 2 (Washington, D.C., 1904), p. 278.

p. 48 *Francis Parkman*: Parkman, *The Oregon Trail*, p. xix.

p. 48 *Among the Cheyennes and Sioux*: see *Wooden Leg: A Warrior Who Fought Custer*, interpreted by Thomas B. Marquis (Lincoln, NE, 1957), pp. 83-87.

p. 50 *"Let us see, is this real"*: quoted in Daniel G. Brinton, *Essays of an Americanist* (Philadelphia, 1890; repr. New York, 1970), p. 292.

p. 50 *"to kill the enemy"*: [Black Hawk], *Life of Ma-ka-tai-me-she-kia-kiak or Black Hawk . . .* (Boston and New York, 1834), p. 47.

p. 50 *"My opinion is"*: Senate and House Debate on Peace with the Indians, *Congressional Globe*, 40th Congress, 1st Session; quoted in Wilcomb E. Washburn, *The American Indian and the United States: A Documentary History*, vol. 2 (New York, 1973), p. 1492.

p. 56 *"Our young men"*: Charles A. Eastman [Ohiyesa], *Indian Boyhood* (New York, 1902), p. 217ff.

p. 57 *"the authorities should see"*: William Abraham Bell, *New Tracks in North America* (London, 1869), pp. 64-65.

p. 57 *"just to show our friends at Washington"*: Albert Barnitz, letter of June 29, 1867, from Camp near Fort Wallace, Kansas; quoted in *Life of Custer's Cavalry: Letters and Diaries of Albert and Jennie Barnitz 1867-1868*, ed. Robert M. Utley (New Haven and London, 1977), p. 74.

p. 59 *"the Sioux came down upon us"*: quoted in Lt. J. Henry Carleton, *The Prairie Logbooks: Dragoon Campaigns to the Pawnee Villages in 1845 and to the Rocky Mountains in 1845*, ed. Louis Pelzer (Lincoln, NE, and London, 1983), pp. 90-91.

PLAINS HUNTERS

p. 61 *"Make the buffalo come"*: quoted in Edwin T. Denig, *Indian Tribes of the Upper Missouri*, 46th Annual Report of the Bureau of American Ethnology, 1928-1929 (Washington, D.C., 1930), p. 484.

p. 62 *The photographer Solomon Carvalho*: see Carvalho, *Incidents of Travel*, p. 113.

p. 70 *While camped peacefully*: Morrow, letter of Oct. 11, 1869; quoted in Hurt and Lass, *Frontier Photographer*, p. 16.

p. 71 *"This was the last place"*: quoted in Brown and Felton, *The Frontier Years*, p. 256.

COUNCIL AT FORT LARAMIE, 1868

p. 75 *"In 1868 men came out"*: from a speech reported in the *New York Times*, July 17, 1870.

p. 78 *"If we want the war"*: Senate and House Debate on Peace with the Indians, *Congressional Globe*, 40th Congress, 1st Session; quoted in Washburn, *The American Indians*, p. 1492.

p. 83 *"You say that"*: quoted in Raymond J. DeMallie, "'Scenes in the Indian Country': A Portfolio of Alexander Gardner's Stereographic Views of the 1868 Fort Laramie Treaty Council," *Montana* 31 (July 1981), p. 47.

p. 84 *"That hereafter no Indian nation"*: Indian Department Appropriations Act, March 3, 1871, *Statutes at Large* 16, pp. 544-45; quoted in Washburn, *The American Indians*, p. 2183.

PAWNEE VILLAGE

p. 87 *"It is too soon to send missionaries"*: quoted in George E. Hyde, *The Pawnee Indians* (Norman, OK, 1974), p. 175.

PUEBLOS

p. 95 *"O our mother the Earth"*: quoted in Herbert J. Spinden, *Songs of the Tewa* (New York, 1933), p. 94.

GHOST DANCERS AND THE MASSACRE AT WOUNDED KNEE, 1890

p. 107 *"The whole world is coming"*: quoted in Mooney, *The Ghost Dance Religion*, p. 1072.

p. 114 *"Indians!"*: quoted in Dee Brown, *Bury My Heart at Wounded Knee* (New York, 1970), p. 431.

p. 117 *"Whatever white men"*: quoted *ibid.*, p. 789.

p. 117 *"outlandish and improbable falsehoods"*: *Chadron Advocate*, Nov. 27, 1890; quoted in Richard E. Jensen, R. Eli Paul, and John E. Carter, *Eyewitness at Wounded Knee* (Lincoln, NE, 1991), p. 45.

p. 118 *"I am an Indian"*: quoted in Julia B. McGillycuddy, *McGillycuddy Agent: A Biography of Dr. Valentine T. McGillycuddy* (Palo Alto, CA, 1941), p. 272.

SELECTED BIBLIOGRAPHY

For literature on individual photographers, see Biographical Notes on the Photographers (pp. 122-30).

Andrews, Ralph W. *Photographers of the Frontier West: Their Lives and Works 1875-1915*. Seattle, 1965.

Andrist, Ralph K. *The Long Death: The Last Days of the Plains Indians*. New York, 1964.

Astrov, Margot, ed. *The Winged Serpent: An Anthology of American Indian Prose and Poetry*. New York, 1946.

Bartlett, Richard H. *Great Surveys of the American West*. Norman, OK, 1962.

Blackman, Margaret. "Posing The American Indian: Early Photographers Often Clothed Reality in Their Own Stereotypes." *Natural History* 89 (1980), pp. 68-74.

————. "Studio Indians: Cartes de Visite of Native People in British Columbia, 1862-1872." *Archivaria* 21 (1986), pp. 68-86.

Bourke, John Gregory. *The Snake Dance of the Moquis of Arizona* . . . New York, 1884.

Brown, Dee. *Bury My Heart at Wounded Knee*. New York, 1970.

Carley, Kenneth. *The Sioux Uprising of 1862*. St. Paul, MN, 1976.

Carvalho, Solomon Nunes. *Incidents of Travel and Adventure in the Far West* . . . (1857). Centenary Edition, ed. and intro. Bertram Wallace Korn. Philadelphia, 1954.

Crawford, William. *The Keepers of the Light: A History and Working Guide to Early Photographic Processes*. Dobbs Ferry, NY, 1979.

Cronyn, George W., ed. *The Path of the Rainbow: An Anthology of Songs and Chants from the Indians of North America*. New York, 1934.

Current, Karen and William R. *Photography and the Old West*. Exhibition catalogue. The Amon Carter Museum of Western Art, Fort Worth, TX. New York, 1978.

Cushing, Frank Hamilton. *Outlines of Zuni Creation Myths*. 13th Annual Report of the Bureau of Ethnology, 1891-1892, pp. 321-447. Washington, D.C., 1896.

————. *My Life in Zuni*. Palo Alto, CA, 1970.

Debo, Angie. *A History of the Indians of the United States*. Norman, OK, 1970.

DeMallie, Raymond J. "'Scenes in the Indian Country': A Portfolio of Alexander Gardner's Stereographic Views of the 1868 Fort Laramie Treaty Council." *Montana* 31 (July 1981), pp. 42-57.

————, and Douglas H. Parks, eds. *Sioux Indian Religion*. Norman, OK, 1987.

Fleming, Paula Richardson, and Judith Luskey. *The North American Indians in Early Photography*. New York, 1986.

Fletcher, Alice C. *Indian Story and Song from North America*. Boston, 1900.

————. *The Hako: A Pawnee Ceremony*. 22nd Annual Report of the Bureau of American Ethnology, 1900-1901, part 2. Washington, D.C., 1904.

Glenn, James. "The 'Curious Gallery': The Indian Photographs of the McClees Studio in Washington, 1857-1858." *History of Photography* 5 (July 1981), pp. 249-62.

Glover, Ridgway. "Photography Among the Indians." *Philadelphia Photographer* 3 (Aug. 1866), pp. 239-40; 3 (Nov. 1866), p. 339; 3 (Dec. 1866), pp. 367-69, 371.

Goetzmann, William. *Exploration and Empire: The Explorer and the Scientist in the Winning of the American West*. New York, 1966.

Gray, John S. "Itinerant Frontier Photographers and Images Lost, Stranded or Stolen." *Montana* 28 (Spring 1978), pp. 2-15.

Grosscup, Jeffrey P. "Stereoscopic Eye on the Frontier West." *Montana* 25 (Spring 1975), pp. 36-50.

Haines, Francis. *The Nez Perces*. Norman, OK, 1955.

Hamilton, Charles. *The Cry of the Thunderbird: The American Indian's Own Story* (1950). Repr. Norman, OK, 1972.

Handbook of North American Indians. Vol. 4: *History of Indian-White Relations*. Ed. Wilcomb E. Washburn. Washington, D.C., 1988. Vols. 9, 10: *Southwest*. Ed. Alfonso Ortiz. Washington, D.C., 1979, 1983.

Hassrick, Royal B. *The Sioux: Life and Customs of a Warrior Society*. Norman, OK, 1964.

Hodge, Frederick, ed. *Handbook of American Indians North of Mexico*. 2 vols. Washington, D.C., 1907, 1910.

Hyde, George. *Red Cloud's Folk: A History of the Oglala Sioux Indians*. Norman, OK, 1975.

Jackson, William H. *Descriptive Catalogue of Photographs of North American Indians*. U.S. Department of Interior Miscellaneous Publication No. 9. Washington, D.C., 1877.

Jensen, Richard E., R. Eli Paul, and John E. Carter. *Eyewitness at Wounded Knee*. Lincoln, NE, 1991.

Johnson, William S., ed. *Nineteenth Century Photography: An Annotated Bibliography, 1839-1879*. Boston and London, 1990.

Joseph, Chief (In-mut-too-yah-lat-lat). "An Indian's View of Indian Affairs." *North American Review* 128 (Apr. 1879), pp. 415-33.

Josephy, Alvin M. *The Patriot Chiefs: A Chronicle of American Indian Resistance*. New York, 1961.

Lowie, Robert H. *Indians of the Plains*. Garden City, NJ, 1963.

Mallery, Garrick. *Pictographs of the North American Indians*. 4th Annual Report of the Bureau of Ethnology, 1882-1883. Washington, D.C., 1886.

Mattison, David, and Daniel Savard. "The North-west Pacific Coast Photographic Voyages 1866-81." *History of Photography* 16 (Autumn 1992), pp. 269-88.

Mooney, James. *The Ghost Dance Religion and the Sioux Outbreak of 1890*. 14th Annual Report of the Bureau of Ethnology 1892-1893, part 2. Washington, D.C., 1896.

Nabakov, Peter, and Robert Easton. *Native American Architecture*. New York and Oxford, 1989.

Naef, Weston J. *Era of Exploration: The Rise of Landscape Photography in the American West, 1860-1885.* Exhibition catalogue. Albright-Knox Art Gallery, Buffalo, NY, and The Metropolitan Museum of Art, New York, 1975.

Neithammer, Carolyn. *Daughters of the Earth: The Lives and Legends of American Indian Women.* New York, 1977.

Newhall, Beaumont. "Minnesota Daguerreotypes." *Minnesota History* 34 (Spring 1954), pp. 28-33.

Nye, Wilbur Sturtevant. *Plains Indian Raiders: The Final Phases of Warfare from the Arkansas to the Red River.* Norman, OK, 1968.

Owen, Roger C., James J. F. Deetz, and Anthony D. Fisher. *The North American Indians: A Sourcebook.* London, 1967.

Palmquist, Peter E. "Imagemakers of the Modoc War: Louis Heller and Eadweard Muybridge." *Journal of California Anthropology* 4 (1977), pp. 206-41.

———. "Photographing the Modoc Indian War: Louis Heller versus Eadweard Muybridge." *History of Photography* 2 (July 1978), pp. 187-205.

———. "The California Indian in Three-Dimensional Photography." *Journal of California and Great Basin Anthropology* 1 (Summer 1979), pp. 89-116.

Papers Relating to Talks and Councils Held with the Indians in Dakota and Montana Territories in the Years 1868-69. Washington, D.C., 1910.

Parsons, E. C. *Pueblo Indian Religion.* Chicago, 1939.

Prucha, Francis Paul. *American Indian Policy in Crisis: Christian Reformers and the Indian 1865-1900.* Norman, OK, 1976.

Rinhart, Floyd and Marion. *The American Daguerreotype.* Athens, GA, 1981.

Scherer, Joanna C. *Indian Images: Photographs of North American Indians 1847-1928.* Exhibition catalogue. Smithsonian Institution, National Anthropological Archives, Washington, D.C., 1970.

———. *Indians: The Great Photographs that Reveal North American Indian Life, 1847-1929, from the Unique Collection of the Smithsonian Institution.* New York, 1973.

———. "You Can't Believe Your Eyes: Inaccuracies in Photographs of North American Indians." *Studies in the Anthropology of Visual Communication* 2 (1975), pp. 67-79.

Snell, Joseph. "Some Rare Western Photographs by Albert Bierstadt now in the Historical Society Collections." *The Kansas Historical Quarterly* 24 (Spring 1958), pp. 1-5.

Standing Bear, Luther. *My People, The Sioux.* Boston, 1928.

———. *My Indian Boyhood.* Boston, 1931.

Stevenson, Matilda Coxe. *The Zuni Indians: Their Mythology, Esoteric Fraternities and Ceremonies.* 23rd Annual Report of the Bureau of American Ethnology, 1901-1902, pp. 3-634. Washington, D.C., 1904.

Taft, Robert. *Photography and the American Scene: A Social History, 1839-1889* (1938). Repr. New York, 1964.

Trennert, Robert A., Jr. "A Grand Failure: The Centennial Indian Exhibition of 1876." *Prologue: The Journal of the National Archives* 6, no. 2 (1974), pp. 118-29.

Utley, Robert M. *The Last Days of the Sioux Nation.* New Haven, 1963.

———. *The Indian Frontier of the American West, 1846-1890.* Albuquerque, 1984.

———. *The Lance and the Shield: The Life and Times of Sitting Bull.* New York, 1993.

Vestal, Stanley. *New Sources of Indian History, 1850-1891.* Norman, OK, 1934.

———. *Sitting Bull: Champion of the Sioux.* Norman, OK, 1957.

Warren, William W. *History of the Ojibways, Based Upon Traditions and Oral Statements.* Collections of the Minnesota Historical Society, vol. 5. St. Paul, MN, 1885.

Washburn, Wilcomb E. *The American Indian and the United States: A Documentary History.* 4 vols. New York, 1973.

Watson, Elmo Scott. "Photographing the Frontier." *The Westerner's Brandbook* (Chicago) 4 (Jan. 1948), pp. 61-63, 65-67.

Weltfish, Gene. *The Lost Universe: The Way of Life of the Pawnee.* New York, 1965.

Wood, Evelyn S. "C. S. Fly of Arizona: The Life and Times of a Frontier Photographer." *History of Photography* 13 (Jan.-Mar. 1989), pp. 31-47.